The Effortless Tower Vortx Dual Basket Air Fryer Cookbook

1500 Days of Quick Healthy and Low-Fat Air Fryer Recipes for Stress-Free and Delicious Mealtimes

Rosemary Cramer

CONTENTS

Bread And Breakfast Recipes

Banana Bread

Servings: 6
Cooking Time: 20 Minutes
Ingredients:

- cooking spray
- 1 cup white wheat flour
- ½ teaspoon baking powder
- ¼ teaspoon salt
- ¼ teaspoon baking soda
- 1 egg
- ½ cup mashed ripe banana
- ¼ cup plain yogurt
- ¼ cup pure maple syrup
- 2 tablespoons coconut oil
- ½ teaspoon pure vanilla extract

Directions:

1. Preheat air fryer to 330°F.
2. Lightly spray 6 x 6-inch baking dish with cooking spray.
3. In a medium bowl, mix together the flour, baking powder, salt, and soda.
4. In a separate bowl, beat the egg and add the mashed banana, yogurt, syrup, oil, and vanilla. Mix until well combined.
5. Pour liquid mixture into dry ingredients and stir gently to blend. Do not beat. Batter may be slightly lumpy.
6. Pour batter into baking dish and cook at 330°F for 20 minutes or until toothpick inserted in center of loaf comes out clean.

Parma Ham & Egg Toast Cups

Servings: 4
Cooking Time: 25 Minutes
Ingredients:

- 4 crusty rolls
- 4 Gouda cheese thin slices
- 5 eggs
- 2 tbsp heavy cream
- ½ tsp dried thyme
- 3 Parma ham slices, chopped
- Salt and pepper to taste

Directions:

1. Preheat air fryer to 330°F. Slice off the top of the rolls, then tear out the insides with your fingers, leaving about ½-inch of bread to make a shell. Press one cheese slice inside the roll shell until it takes the shape of the roll.
2. Beat eggs with heavy cream in a medium bowl. Next, mix in the remaining ingredients. Spoon egg mixture into the rolls lined with cheese. Place rolls in the greased frying basket and Bake until eggs are puffy and brown, 8-12 minutes. Serve warm.

Tuscan Toast

Servings: 4
Cooking Time: 5 Minutes
Ingredients:

- ¼ cup butter
- ½ teaspoon lemon juice
- ½ clove garlic
- ½ teaspoon dried parsley flakes
- 4 slices Italian bread, 1-inch thick

Directions:

1. Place butter, lemon juice, garlic, and parsley in a food processor. Process about 1 minute, or until garlic is pulverized and ingredients are well blended.
2. Spread garlic butter on both sides of bread slices.
3. Place bread slices upright in air fryer basket. (They can lie flat but cook better standing on end.)
4. Cook at 390°F for 5minutes or until toasty brown.

Crunchy French Toast Sticks

Servings: 2
Cooking Time: 9 Minutes
Ingredients:

- 2 eggs, beaten
- ¾ cup milk
- ½ teaspoon vanilla extract
- ½ teaspoon ground cinnamon
- 1½ cups crushed crunchy cinnamon cereal, or any cereal flakes
- 4 slices Texas Toast (or other bread that you can slice into 1-inch thick slices)
- maple syrup, for serving
- vegetable oil or melted butter

Directions:

1. Combine the eggs, milk, vanilla and cinnamon in a shallow bowl. Place the crushed cereal in a second shallow bowl.
2. Trim the crusts off the slices of bread and cut each slice into 3 sticks. Dip the sticks of bread into the egg

mixture, turning them over to coat all sides. Let the bread sticks absorb the egg mixture for ten seconds or so, but don't let them get too wet. Roll the bread sticks in the cereal crumbs, pressing the cereal gently onto all sides so that it adheres to the bread.

3. Preheat the air fryer to 400°F.
4. Spray or brush the air fryer basket with oil or melted butter. Place the coated sticks in the basket. It's ok to stack a few on top of the others in the opposite direction.
5. Air-fry for 9 minutes. Turn the sticks over a couple of times during the cooking process so that the sticks crisp evenly. Serve warm with the maple syrup or some berries.

Seafood Quinoa Frittata

Servings: 4
Cooking Time: 30 Minutes

Ingredients:

- ½ cup cooked shrimp, chopped
- ½ cup cooked quinoa
- ½ cup baby spinach
- 4 eggs
- ½ tsp dried basil
- 1 anchovy, chopped
- ½ cup grated cheddar

Directions:

1. Preheat air fryer to 320°F. Add quinoa, shrimp, and spinach to a greased baking pan. Set aside. Beat eggs, anchovy, and basil in a bowl until frothy. Pour over the quinoa mixture, then top with cheddar cheese. Bake until the frittata is puffed and golden, 14-18 minutes. Serve.

Orange Rolls

Servings: 8
Cooking Time: 10 Minutes

Ingredients:

- parchment paper
- 3 ounces low-fat cream cheese
- 1 tablespoon low-fat sour cream or plain yogurt (not Greek yogurt)
- 2 teaspoons sugar
- ¼ teaspoon pure vanilla extract
- ¼ teaspoon orange extract
- 1 can (8 count) organic crescent roll dough
- ¼ cup chopped walnuts
- ¼ cup dried cranberries
- ¼ cup shredded, sweetened coconut
- butter-flavored cooking spray
- Orange Glaze
- ½ cup powdered sugar
- 1 tablespoon orange juice
- ¼ teaspoon orange extract
- dash of salt

Directions:

1. Cut a circular piece of parchment paper slightly smaller than the bottom of your air fryer basket. Set aside.
2. In a small bowl, combine the cream cheese, sour cream or yogurt, sugar, and vanilla and orange extracts. Stir until smooth.
3. Preheat air fryer to 300°F.
4. Separate crescent roll dough into 8 triangles and divide cream cheese mixture among them. Starting at wide end, spread cheese mixture to within 1 inch of point.
5. Sprinkle nuts and cranberries evenly over cheese mixture.
6. Starting at wide end, roll up triangles, then sprinkle with coconut, pressing in lightly to make it stick. Spray tops of rolls with butter-flavored cooking spray.
7. Place parchment paper in air fryer basket, and place 4 rolls on top, spaced evenly.
8. Cook for 10minutes, until rolls are golden brown and cooked through.
9. Repeat steps 7 and 8 to cook remaining 4 rolls. You should be able to use the same piece of parchment paper twice.
10. In a small bowl, stir together ingredients for glaze and drizzle over warm rolls.

Seasoned Herbed Sourdough Croutons

Servings: 4
Cooking Time: 7 Minutes

Ingredients:

- 4 cups cubed sourdough bread, 1-inch cubes (about 8 ounces)
- 1 tablespoon olive oil
- 1 teaspoon fresh thyme leaves
- ¼ – ½ teaspoon salt
- freshly ground black pepper

Directions:

1. Combine all ingredients in a bowl and taste to make sure it is seasoned to your liking.
2. Preheat the air fryer to 400°F.
3. Toss the bread cubes into the air fryer and air-fry for 7 minutes, shaking the basket once or twice while they cook.
4. Serve warm or store in an airtight container.

Mashed Potato Taquitos With Hot Sauce

Servings: 4

Cooking Time: 30 Minutes

Ingredients:

- 1 potato, peeled and cubed
- 2 tbsp milk
- 2 garlic cloves, minced
- Salt and pepper to taste
- ½ tsp ground cumin
- 2 tbsp minced scallions
- 4 corn tortillas
- 1 cup red chili sauce
- 1 avocado, sliced
- 2 tbsp cilantro, chopped

Directions:

1. In a pot fitted with a steamer basket, cook the potato cubes for 15 minutes on the stovetop. Pour the potato cubes into a bowl and mash with a potato masher. Add the milk, garlic, salt, pepper, and cumin and stir. Add the scallions and cilantro and stir them into the mixture.
2. Preheat air fryer to 390°F. Run the tortillas under water for a second, then place them in the greased frying basket. Air Fry for 1 minute. Lay the tortillas on a flat surface. Place an equal amount of the potato filling in the center of each. Roll the tortilla sides over the filling and place seam-side down in the frying basket. Fry for 7 minutes or until the tortillas are golden and slightly crisp. Serve with chili sauce and avocado slices. Enjoy!

Carrot Muffins

Servings: 4

Cooking Time: 35 Minutes + Cooling Time

Ingredients:

- 1 ½ cups flour
- ½ tsp baking soda
- ½ tsp baking powder
- 1/3 cup brown sugar
- ½ tsp ground cinnamon
- 2 eggs
- 2/3 cup almond milk
- 3 tbsp sunflower oil
- ½ cup shredded carrots
- 1/3 cup golden raisins

Directions:

1. Preheat air fryer to 320°F. Mix the flour, baking powder, baking soda, brown sugar, and cinnamon in a bowl. In a smaller bowl, whisk the eggs, almond milk, and oil. Combine the mixtures, stir, but leave some lumps in the batter. Add the carrots and raisins and stir. Make 8 foil muffin cups by doubling 16 cups. Set 4 cups in the air fryer and put the batter in the cups until they're ¾ full. Bake in the fryer for 13-17 minutes; the muffin tops should bounce when touched. Repeat until all muffins are done. Let the muffins cool on a rack, then serve.

French Toast Sticks

Servings: 4

Cooking Time: 7 Minutes

Ingredients:

- 2 eggs
- ½ cup milk
- ⅛ teaspoon salt
- ½ teaspoon pure vanilla extract
- ¾ cup crushed cornflakes
- 6 slices sandwich bread, each slice cut into 4 strips
- oil for misting or cooking spray
- maple syrup or honey

Directions:

1. In a small bowl, beat together eggs, milk, salt, and vanilla.
2. Place crushed cornflakes on a plate or in a shallow dish.
3. Dip bread strips in egg mixture, shake off excess, and roll in cornflake crumbs.
4. Spray both sides of bread strips with oil.
5. Place bread strips in air fryer basket in single layer.
6. Cook at 390°F for 7minutes or until they're dark golden brown.
7. Repeat steps 5 and 6 to cook remaining French toast sticks.
8. Serve with maple syrup or honey for dipping.

Eggless Mung Bean Tart

Servings: 2
Cooking Time: 20 Minutes

Ingredients:

- 2 tsp soy sauce
- 1 tsp lime juice
- 1 large garlic clove, minced or pressed
- ½ tsp red chili flakes
- ½ cup mung beans, soaked
- Salt and pepper to taste
- ½ minced shallot
- 1 green onion, chopped

Directions:

1. Preheat the air fryer to 390°F. Add the soy sauce, lime juice, garlic, and chili flakes to a bowl and stir. Set aside.Place the drained beans in a blender along with ½ cup of water, salt, and pepper. Blend until smooth. Stir in shallot and green onion, but do not blend.
2. Pour the batter into a greased baking pan. Bake for 15 minutes in the air fryer until golden. A knife inserted in the center should come out clean. Once cooked, cut the "quiche" into quarters. Drizzle with sauce and serve.

English Breakfast

Servings: 2
Cooking Time: 30 Minutes

Ingredients:

- 6 bacon strips
- 1 cup cooked white beans
- 1 tbsp melted butter
- ½ tbsp flour
- Salt and pepper to taste
- 2 eggs

Directions:

1. Preheat air fryer to 360°F. In a second bowl, combine the beans, butter, flour, salt, and pepper. Mix well. Put the bacon in the frying basket and Air Fry for 10 minutes, flipping once. Remove the bacon and stir in the beans. Crack the eggs on top and cook for 10-12 minutes until the eggs are set. Serve with bacon.

Lime Muffins

Servings: 6
Cooking Time: 30 Minutes

Ingredients:

- 1 ½ tbsp butter, softened
- 6 tbsp sugar
- 1 egg
- 1 egg white
- 1 tsp vanilla extract
- 1 tsp lime juice
- 1 lime, zested
- 5 oz Greek yogurt
- ¾ cup + 2 tbsp flour
- ¾ cup raspberries

Directions:

1. Beat butter and sugar in a mixer for 2 minutes at medium speed. In a separate bowl, whisk together the egg, egg white and vanilla. Pour into the mixer bowl, add lime juice and zest. Beat until combined. At a low speed, add yogurt then flour. Fold in the raspberries. Divide the mixture into 6 greased muffin cups using an ice cream scoop. The cups should be filled about ¾ of the way.
2. Preheat air fryer to 300°F. Put the muffins into the air fryer and Bake for 15 minutes until the tops are golden and a toothpick in the center comes out clean. Allow to cool before serving.

Garlic Parmesan Bread Ring

Servings: 6
Cooking Time: 30 Minutes

Ingredients:

- ½ cup unsalted butter, melted
- ¼ teaspoon salt (omit if using salted butter)
- ¾ cup grated Parmesan cheese
- 3 to 4 cloves garlic, minced
- 1 tablespoon chopped fresh parsley
- 1 pound frozen bread dough, defrosted
- olive oil
- 1 egg, beaten

Directions:

1. Combine the melted butter, salt, Parmesan cheese, garlic and chopped parsley in a small bowl.
2. Roll the dough out into a rectangle that measures 8 inches by 17 inches. Spread the butter mixture over the dough, leaving a half-inch border un-buttered along one of the long edges. Roll the dough from one long edge to the other, ending with the un-buttered border. Pinch the seam shut tightly. Shape the log into a circle sealing the ends together by pushing one end into the other and stretching the dough around it.
3. Cut out a circle of aluminum foil that is the same size as the air fryer basket. Brush the foil circle with oil and place an oven safe ramekin or glass in the center. Transfer the dough ring to the aluminum foil circle, around the ramekin. This will help you make sure the dough will fit in the basket and maintain its ring shape.

Use kitchen shears to cut 8 slits around the outer edge of the dough ring halfway to the center. Brush the dough ring with egg wash.

4. Preheat the air fryer to 400°F for 4 minutes. When it has Preheated, brush the sides of the basket with oil and transfer the dough ring, foil circle and ramekin into the basket. Slide the drawer back into the air fryer, but do not turn the air fryer on. Let the dough rise inside the warm air fryer for 30 minutes.

5. After the bread has proofed in the air fryer for 30 minutes, set the temperature to 340°F and air-fry the bread ring for 15 minutes. Flip the bread over by inverting it onto a plate or cutting board and sliding it back into the air fryer basket. Air-fry for another 15 minutes. Let the bread cool for a few minutes before slicing the bread ring in between the slits and serving warm.

Bagels With Avocado & Tomatoes

Servings: 2

Cooking Time: 35 Minutes

Ingredients:

- 2/3 cup all-purpose flour
- ½ tsp active dry yeast
- 1/3 cup Greek yogurt
- 8 cherry tomatoes
- 1 ripe avocado
- 1 tbsp lemon juice
- 2 tbsp chopped red onions
- Black pepper to taste

Directions:

1. Preheat air fryer to 400°F. Beat the flour, dry yeast, and Greek yogurt until you get a smooth dough, adding more flour if necessary. Make 2 equal balls out of the mixture.
2. Using a rolling pin, roll each ball into a 9-inch long strip. Form a ring with each strip and press the ends together to create 2 bagels. In a bowl with hot water, soak the bagels for 1 minute. Shake excess water and let rise for 15 minutes in the fryer. Bake for 5 minutes, turn the bagels, top with tomatoes, and Bake for another 5 minutes.
3. Cut avocado in half, discard the pit and remove the flesh into a bowl. Mash with a fork and stir in lemon juice and onions. Once the bagels are ready, let cool slightly and cut them in half. Spread on each half some guacamole, top with 2 slices of Baked tomatoes, and sprinkle with pepper. Serve immediately.

Orange Cran-bran Muffins

Servings: 4

Cooking Time: 30 Minutes

Ingredients:

- 1 ½ cups bran cereal flakes
- 1 cup flour
- 3 tbsp granulated sugar
- 1 tbsp orange zest
- 1 tsp baking powder
- 1 cup milk
- 3 tbsp peanut oil
- 1 egg
- ½ cup dried cranberries

Directions:

1. Preheat air fryer to 320°F. Combine the cereal, flour, granulated sugar, orange zest, and baking powder in a bowl, and in another bowl, beat the milk, oil, and egg. Add the egg mix to the dry ingredients and stir, then add the cranberries and stir again. Make 8 foil muffin cups by doubling 16 cups. Set 4 cups in the frying basket and spoon the batter in the cups until they're ¾ full. Bake for 15 minutes or until the tops bounce when touched. Set the muffins on a wire rack for 10 minutes, then serve.

Smooth Walnut-banana Loaf

Servings: 4

Cooking Time: 40 Minutes

Ingredients:

- 1/3 cup peanut butter, melted
- 2 tbsp butter, melted and cooled
- ¾ cup flour
- ½ tsp salt
- ¼ tsp baking soda
- 2 ripe bananas
- 2 eggs
- 1 tsp lemon juice
- ½ cup evaporated cane sugar
- ½ cup ground walnuts
- 1 tbsp blackstrap molasses
- 1 tsp vanilla extract

Directions:

1. Preheat air fryer to 310°F. Mix flour, salt, and baking soda in a small bowl. Mash together bananas and eggs in a large bowl, then stir in sugar, peanut butter, lemon juice, butter, walnuts, molasses, and vanilla. When it is well incorporated, stir in the flour mixture until just combined. Transfer the batter to a

parchment-lined baking dish and make sure it is even. Bake in the air fryer for 30 to 35 minutes until a toothpick in the middle comes out clean, and the top is golden. Serve and enjoy.

Crispy Chicken Cakes

Servings: 4
Cooking Time: 30 Minutes
Ingredients:

- 1 peeled Granny Smith apple, chopped
- 2 scallions, chopped
- 3 tbsp ground almonds
- 1 tsp garlic powder
- 1 egg white
- 2 tbsp apple juice
- Black pepper to taste
- 1 lb ground chicken

Directions:

1. Preheat air fryer to 330°F. Combine the apple, scallions, almonds, garlic powder, egg white, apple juice, and pepper in a bowl. Add the ground chicken using your hands. Mix well. Make 8 patties and set four in the frying basket. Air Fry for 8-12 minutes until crispy. Repeat with the remaining patties. Serve hot.

Blueberry Pannenkoek (dutch Pancake)

Servings: 4
Cooking Time: 30 Minutes
Ingredients:

- 3 eggs, beaten
- ½ cup buckwheat flour
- ½ cup milk
- ½ tsp vanilla
- 1 ½ cups blueberries, crushed
- 2 tbsp powdered sugar

Directions:

1. Preheat air fryer to 330°F. Mix together eggs, buckwheat flour, milk, and vanilla in a bowl. Pour the batter into a greased baking pan and add it to the fryer. Bake until the pancake is puffed and golden, 12-16 minutes. Remove the pan and flip the pancake over onto a plate. Add blueberries and powdered sugar as a topping and serve.

Cherry-apple Oatmeal Cups

Servings: 2
Cooking Time: 20 Minutes
Ingredients:

- 2/3 cup rolled oats
- 1 cored apple, diced
- 4 pitted cherries, diced
- ½ tsp ground cinnamon
- ¾ cup milk

Directions:

1. Preheat air fryer to 350°F. Mix the oats, apple, cherries, and cinnamon in a heatproof bowl. Add in milk and Bake for 6 minutes, stir well and Bake for 6 more minutes until the fruit are soft. Serve cooled.

Crispy Bacon

Servings: 6
Cooking Time: 20 Minutes
Ingredients:

- 12 ounces bacon

Directions:

1. Preheat the air fryer to 350°F for 3 minutes.
2. Lay out the bacon in a single layer, slightly overlapping the strips of bacon.
3. Air fry for 10 minutes or until desired crispness.
4. Repeat until all the bacon has been cooked.

Nordic Salmon Quiche

Servings: 4
Cooking Time: 30 Minutes
Ingredients:

- ¼ cup shredded mozzarella cheese
- ¼ cup shredded Gruyere cheese
- 1 refrigerated pie crust
- 2 eggs
- ¼ cup milk
- Salt and pepper to taste
- 1 tsp dry dill
- 5 oz cooked salmon
- 1 large tomato, diced

Directions:

1. Preheat air fryer to 360°F. In a baking dish, add the crust and press firmly. Trim off any excess edges. Poke a few holes. Beat the eggs in a bowl. Stir in the milk, dill, tomato, salmon, half of the cheeses, salt, and pepper. Mix well as break the salmon into chunks, mixing it evenly among other ingredients. Transfer the mix to the baking dish.
2. Bake in the fryer for 15 minutes until firm and almost crusty. Slide the basket out and top with the remaining cheeses. Cook further for 5 minutes, or until golden brown. Let cool slightly and serve.

Wild Blueberry Lemon Chia Bread

Servings: 6
Cooking Time: 27 Minutes
Ingredients:

- ¼ cup extra-virgin olive oil
- ⅓ cup plus 1 tablespoon cane sugar
- 1 large egg
- 3 tablespoons fresh lemon juice
- 1 tablespoon lemon zest
- ⅔ cup milk
- 1 cup all-purpose flour
- ¾ teaspoon baking powder
- ⅛ teaspoon salt
- 2 tablespoons chia seeds
- 1 cup frozen wild blueberries
- ⅓ cup powdered sugar
- 2 teaspoons milk

Directions:

1. Preheat the air fryer to 310°F.
2. In a medium bowl, mix the olive oil with the sugar. Whisk in the egg, lemon juice, lemon zest, and milk; set aside.
3. In a small bowl, combine the all-purpose flour, baking powder, and salt.
4. Slowly mix the dry ingredients into the wet ingredients. Stir in the chia seeds and wild blueberries.
5. Liberally spray a 7-inch springform pan with olive-oil spray. Pour the batter into the pan and place the pan in the air fryer. Bake for 25 to 27 minutes, or until a toothpick inserted in the center comes out clean.
6. Remove and let cool on a wire rack for 10 minutes prior to removing from the pan.
7. Meanwhile, in a small bowl, mix the powdered sugar with the milk to create the glaze.
8. Slice and serve with a drizzle of the powdered sugar glaze.

Pancake Muffins

Servings: 4
Cooking Time: 8 Minutes
Ingredients:

- 1 cup flour
- 2 tablespoons sugar (optional)
- ½ teaspoon baking soda
- 1 teaspoon baking powder
- ¼ teaspoon salt
- 1 egg, beaten
- 1 cup buttermilk
- 2 tablespoons melted butter
- 1 teaspoon pure vanilla extract
- 24 foil muffin cups
- cooking spray
- Suggested Fillings
- 1 teaspoon of jelly or fruit preserves
- 1 tablespoon or less fresh blueberries; chopped fresh strawberries; chopped frozen cherries; dark chocolate chips; chopped walnuts, pecans, or other nuts; cooked, crumbled bacon or sausage

Directions:

1. In a large bowl, stir together flour, optional sugar, baking soda, baking powder, and salt.
2. In a small bowl, combine egg, buttermilk, butter, and vanilla. Mix well.
3. Pour egg mixture into dry ingredients and stir to mix well but don't overbeat.
4. Double up the muffin cups and remove the paper liners from the top cups. Spray the foil cups lightly with cooking spray.
5. Place 6 sets of muffin cups in air fryer basket. Pour just enough batter into each cup to cover the bottom. Sprinkle with desired filling. Pour in more batter to cover the filling and fill the cups about ¾ full.
6. Cook at 330°F for 8minutes.
7. Repeat steps 5 and 6 for the remaining 6 pancake muffins.

Apple & Turkey Breakfast Sausages

Servings: 4
Cooking Time: 15 Minutes
Ingredients:

- ½ tsp coriander seeds, crushed
- 1 tbsp chopped rosemary
- 1 tbsp chopped thyme
- Salt and pepper to taste
- 1 tsp fennel seeds, crushed
- ¾ tsp smoked paprika
- ½ tsp garlic powder
- ½ tsp shallot powder
- ⅛ tsp red pepper flakes
- 1 pound ground turkey
- ½ cup minced apples

Directions:

1. Combine all of the seasonings in a bowl. Add turkey and apple and blend seasonings in well with

your hands. Form patties about 3 inches in diameter and 1/4 inch thick.

2. Preheat air fryer to 400°F. Arrange patties in a single layer on the greased frying basket. Air Fry for 10 minutes, flipping once until brown and cooked through. Serve.

Roasted Vegetable Frittata

Servings: 1

Cooking Time: 19 Minutes

Ingredients:

- 1/2 red or green bell pepper, cut into 1/2-inch chunks
- 4 button mushrooms, sliced
- 1/2 cup diced zucchini
- 1/2 teaspoon chopped fresh oregano or thyme
- 1 teaspoon olive oil
- 3 eggs, beaten
- 1/2 cup grated Cheddar cheese
- salt and freshly ground black pepper, to taste
- 1 teaspoon butter
- 1 teaspoon chopped fresh parsley

Directions:

1. Preheat the air fryer to 400°F.
2. Toss the peppers, mushrooms, zucchini and oregano with the olive oil and air-fry for 6 minutes, shaking the basket once or twice during the cooking process to redistribute the ingredients.
3. While the vegetables are cooking, beat the eggs well in a bowl, stir in the Cheddar cheese and season with salt and freshly ground black pepper. Add the air-fried vegetables to this bowl when they have finished cooking.
4. Place a 6- or 7-inch non-stick metal cake pan into the air fryer basket with the butter using an aluminum sling to lower the pan into the basket. (Fold a piece of aluminum foil into a strip about 2-inches wide by 24-inches long.) Air-fry for 1 minute at 380°F to melt the butter. Remove the cake pan and rotate the pan to distribute the butter and grease the pan. Pour the egg mixture into the cake pan and return the pan to the air fryer, using the aluminum sling.
5. Air-fry at 380°F for 12 minutes, or until the frittata has puffed up and is lightly browned. Let the frittata sit in the air fryer for 5 minutes to cool to an edible temperature and set up. Remove the cake pan from the air fryer, sprinkle with parsley and serve immediately.

Garlic-cheese Biscuits

Servings: 8

Cooking Time: 8 Minutes

Ingredients:

- 1 cup self-rising flour
- 1 teaspoon garlic powder
- 2 tablespoons butter, diced
- 2 ounces sharp Cheddar cheese, grated
- 1/2 cup milk
- cooking spray

Directions:

1. Preheat air fryer to 330°F.
2. Combine flour and garlic in a medium bowl and stir together.
3. Using a pastry blender or knives, cut butter into dry ingredients.
4. Stir in cheese.
5. Add milk and stir until stiff dough forms.
6. If dough is too sticky to handle, stir in 1 or 2 more tablespoons of self-rising flour before shaping. Biscuits should be firm enough to hold their shape. Otherwise, they'll stick to the air fryer basket.
7. Divide dough into 8 portions and shape into 2-inch biscuits about 3/4-inch thick.
8. Spray air fryer basket with nonstick cooking spray.
9. Place all 8 biscuits in basket and cook at 330°F for 8 minutes.

Quiche Cups

Servings: 10

Cooking Time: 16 Minutes

Ingredients:

- 1/4 pound all-natural ground pork sausage
- 3 eggs
- 3/4 cup milk
- 20 foil muffin cups
- cooking spray
- 4 ounces sharp Cheddar cheese, grated

Directions:

1. Divide sausage into 3 portions and shape each into a thin patty.
2. Place patties in air fryer basket and cook 390°F for 6minutes.
3. While sausage is cooking, prepare the egg mixture. A large measuring cup or bowl with a pouring lip works best. Combine the eggs and milk and whisk until well blended. Set aside.
4. When sausage has cooked fully, remove patties from basket, drain well, and use a fork to crumble the meat into small pieces.

5. Double the foil cups into 10 sets. Remove paper liners from the top muffin cups and spray the foil cups lightly with cooking spray.
6. Divide crumbled sausage among the 10 muffin cup sets.
7. Top each with grated cheese, divided evenly among the cups.
8. Place 5 cups in air fryer basket.
9. Pour egg mixture into each cup, filling until each cup is at least ⅔ full.
10. Cook for 8 minutes and test for doneness. A knife inserted into the center shouldn't have any raw egg on it when removed.
11. If needed, cook 2 more minutes, until egg completely sets.
12. Repeat steps 8 through 11 for the remaining quiches.

Cheddar-ham-corn Muffins

Servings: 8
Cooking Time: 8 Minutes
Ingredients:

- ¾ cup yellow cornmeal
- ¼ cup flour
- 1½ teaspoons baking powder
- ¼ teaspoon salt
- 1 egg, beaten
- 2 tablespoons canola oil
- ½ cup milk
- ½ cup shredded sharp Cheddar cheese
- ½ cup diced ham
- 8 foil muffin cups, liners removed and sprayed with cooking spray

Directions:

1. Preheat air fryer to 390°F.
2. In a medium bowl, stir together the cornmeal, flour, baking powder, and salt.
3. Add egg, oil, and milk to dry ingredients and mix well.
4. Stir in shredded cheese and diced ham.
5. Divide batter among the muffin cups.
6. Place 4 filled muffin cups in air fryer basket and bake for 5minutes.
7. Reduce temperature to 330°F and bake for 1 to 2minutes or until toothpick inserted in center of muffin comes out clean.
8. Repeat steps 6 and 7 to cook remaining muffins.

Meaty Omelet

Servings: 4
Cooking Time: 20 Minutes
Ingredients:

- 6 eggs
- ½ cup grated Swiss cheese
- 3 breakfast sausages, sliced
- 8 bacon strips, sliced
- Salt and pepper to taste

Directions:

1. Preheat air fryer to 360°F. In a bowl, beat the eggs and stir in Swiss cheese, sausages and bacon. Transfer the mixture to a baking dish and set in the fryer. Bake for 15 minutes or until golden and crisp. Season and serve.

Shakshuka-style Pepper Cups

Servings:4
Cooking Time: 35 Minutes
Ingredients:

- 2 tbsp ricotta cheese crumbles
- 1 tbsp olive oil
- ½ yellow onion, diced
- 2 cloves garlic, minced
- ¼ tsp turmeric
- 1 can diced tomatoes
- 1 tbsp tomato paste
- ½ tsp smoked paprika
- ½ tsp salt
- ½ tsp granular sugar
- ¼ tsp ground cumin
- ¼ tsp ground coriander
- ⅛ tsp cayenne pepper
- 4 bell peppers
- 4 eggs
- 2 tbsp chopped basil

Directions:

1. Warm the olive oil in a saucepan over medium heat. Stir-fry the onion for 10 minutes or until softened. Stir in the garlic and turmeric for another 1 minute. Add diced tomatoes, tomato paste, paprika, salt, sugar, cumin, coriander, and cayenne. Remove from heat and stir.
2. Preheat air fryer to 350°F. Slice the tops off the peppers, and carefully remove the core and seeds. Put the bell peppers in the frying basket. Divide the tomato mixture among bell peppers. Crack 1 egg into tomato mixture in each pepper. Bake for 8-10 minutes. Sprinkle with ricotta cheese and cook for 1 more minute. Let rest 5 minutes. Garnish with fresh basil and serve immediately.

Egg & Bacon Pockets

Servings: 4
Cooking Time: 50 Minutes
Ingredients:

- 2 tbsp olive oil
- 4 bacon slices, chopped
- ¼ red bell pepper, diced
- 1/3 cup scallions, chopped
- 4 eggs, beaten
- 1/3 cup grated Swiss cheese
- 1 cup flour
- 1 ½ tsp baking powder
- ½ tsp salt
- 1 cup Greek yogurt
- 1 egg white, beaten
- 2 tsp Italian seasoning
- 1 tbsp Tabasco sauce

Directions:

1. Warm the olive oil in a skillet over medium heat and add the bacon. Stir-fry for 3-4 minutes or until crispy. Add the bell pepper and scallions and sauté for 3-4 minutes. Pour in the beaten eggs and stir-fry to scramble them, 3 minutes. Stir in the Swiss cheese and set aside to cool.
2. Sift the flour, baking powder, and salt in a bowl. Add yogurt and mix together until combined. Transfer the dough to a floured workspace. Knead it for 3 minutes or until smooth. Form the dough into 4 equal balls. Roll out the balls into round discs. Divide the bacon-egg mixture between the rounds. Fold the dough over the filling and seal the edges with a fork. Brush the pockets with egg white and sprinkle with Italian seasoning.
3. Preheat air fryer to 350°F. Arrange the pockets on the greased frying basket and Bake for 9-11 minutes, flipping once until golden. Serve with Tabasco sauce.

Blueberry Applesauce Oat Cake

Servings: 4
Cooking Time: 65 Minutes
Ingredients:

- 1 cup applesauce
- 2/3 cup quick-cooking oats
- ½ tsp baking powder
- A pinch of salt
- ½ cup almond milk
- 5 tbsp almond flour
- 1 tbsp honey
- 1 egg
- 1 tsp vanilla extract
- ½ cup blueberries
- 4 tbsp grape preserves

Directions:

1. In a bowl, combine oats, baking powder, and salt. In a larger bowl, combine milk, almond flour, honey, egg, and vanilla with a whisk until well mixed. Add the applesauce until combined, then add the oat mixture. Gently fold in blueberries. Pour the mixture into a greased baking dish. Spoon jelly over the top, but do not stir it in.
2. Preheat air fryer to 300°F. Put the baking dish into the air fryer. Bake until the top is golden and the oatmeal is set, 25 minutes. Remove and allow to cool for 10-15 minutes. Slice four ways and serve warm.

Seedy Bagels

Servings: 4
Cooking Time: 25 Minutes
Ingredients:

- 1 ¼ cups flour
- 2 tsp baking powder
- ½ tsp salt
- 1 cup plain Greek yogurt
- 1 egg
- 1 tsp water
- 1 tsp poppy seeds
- ½ tsp white sesame seeds
- ½ tsp black sesame seeds
- ½ tsp coriander seeds
- 1 tsp cumin powder
- ½ tsp dried minced onion
- 1 tsp coarse salt

Directions:

1. Preheat air fryer to 300°F. Mix 1 cup flour, baking powder, salt, and cumin in a bowl. Stir in yogurt until a sticky dough forms. Separate the dough into 4 equal portions. Dust a flat work surface with ¼ cup flour. Roll out each portion of dough into a 6-inch log. Pull the two ends around to meet and press the ends together to seal.
2. Whisk egg and water in a small bowl. Prepare the topping in another small bowl by combining poppy seeds, white sesame seeds, black sesame seeds, coriander seeds, minced onion, and salt. Brush the egg wash on the bagel tops and sprinkle with the topping. Transfer to the frying basket and bake for 12 to 15 minutes until the tops are golden. Serve and enjoy.

Banana-strawberry Cakecups

Servings: 6
Cooking Time: 25 Minutes
Ingredients:

- ½ cup mashed bananas
- ¼ cup maple syrup
- ½ cup Greek yogurt
- 1 tsp vanilla extract
- 1 egg
- 1 ½ cups flour
- 1 tbsp cornstarch
- ½ tsp baking soda
- ½ tsp baking powder
- ½ tsp salt
- ½ cup strawberries, sliced

Directions:

1. Preheat air fryer to 360°F. Place the mashed bananas, maple syrup, yogurt, vanilla, and egg in a large bowl and mix until smooth. Sift in 1 ½ cups of the flour, baking soda, baking powder, and salt, then stir to combine.
2. In a small bowl, toss the strawberries with the cornstarch. Fold the mixture into the muffin batter. Divide the mixture evenly between greased muffin cups and place into the air frying basket. Bake for 12-15 minutes until golden brown on top and a toothpick inserted into the middle of one of the muffins comes out clean. Leave to cool for 5 minutes. Serve and enjoy!

Cheesy Egg Popovers

Servings:6
Cooking Time: 30 Minutes
Ingredients:

- 5 eggs
- 1 tbsp milk
- 2 tbsp heavy cream
- Salt and pepper to taste
- ⅛ tsp ground nutmeg
- ¼ cup grated Swiss cheese

Directions:

1. Preheat air fryer to 350°F. Beat all ingredients in a bowl. Divide between greased muffin cups and place them in the frying basket. Bake for 9 minutes. Let cool slightly before serving.

Peppered Maple Bacon Knots

Servings: 6
Cooking Time: 8 Minutes
Ingredients:

- 1 pound maple smoked center-cut bacon
- ¼ cup maple syrup
- ¼ cup brown sugar
- coarsely cracked black peppercorns

Directions:

1. Tie each bacon strip in a loose knot and place them on a baking sheet.
2. Combine the maple syrup and brown sugar in a bowl. Brush each knot generously with this mixture and sprinkle with coarsely cracked black pepper.
3. Preheat the air fryer to 390°F.
4. Air-fry the bacon knots in batches. Place one layer of knots in the air fryer basket and air-fry for 5 minutes. Turn the bacon knots over and air-fry for an additional 3 minutes.
5. Serve warm.

Lemon-blueberry Morning Bread

Servings:2
Cooking Time: 15 Minutes
Ingredients:

- ½ cup flour
- ¼ cup powdered sugar
- ½ tsp baking powder
- ⅛ tsp salt
- 2 tbsp butter, melted
- 1 egg
- ½ tsp gelatin
- ½ tsp vanilla extract
- 1 tsp lemon zest
- ½ cup blueberries

Directions:

1. Preheat air fryer to 300°F. Mix the flour, sugar, baking powder, and salt in a bowl. In another bowl, whisk the butter, egg, gelatin, lemon zest, vanilla extract, and blueberries. Add egg mixture to flour mixture and stir until smooth. Spoon mixture into a pizza pan. Place pan in the frying basket and Bake for 10 minutes. Let sit for 5 minutes before slicing. Serve immediately.

Hashbrown Potatoes Lyonnaise

Servings: 4
Cooking Time: 33 Minutes

Ingredients:

- 1 Vidalia (or other sweet) onion, sliced
- 1 teaspoon butter, melted
- 1 teaspoon brown sugar
- 2 large russet potatoes (about 1 pound), sliced ½-inch thick
- 1 tablespoon vegetable oil
- salt and freshly ground black pepper

Directions:

1. Preheat the air fryer to 370°F.
2. Toss the sliced onions, melted butter and brown sugar together in the air fryer basket. Air-fry for 8 minutes, shaking the basket occasionally to help the onions cook evenly.
3. While the onions are cooking, bring a 3-quart saucepan of salted water to a boil on the stovetop. Par-cook the potatoes in boiling water for 3 minutes. Drain the potatoes and pat them dry with a clean kitchen towel.
4. Add the potatoes to the onions in the air fryer basket and drizzle with vegetable oil. Toss to coat the potatoes with the oil and season with salt and freshly ground black pepper.
5. Increase the air fryer temperature to 400°F and air-fry for 22 minutes tossing the vegetables a few times during the cooking time to help the potatoes brown evenly. Season to taste again with salt and freshly ground black pepper and serve warm.

Tri-color Frittata

Servings: 4
Cooking Time: 30 Minutes

Ingredients:

- 8 eggs, beaten
- 1 red bell pepper, diced
- Salt and pepper to taste
- 1 garlic clove, minced
- ½ tsp dried oregano
- ½ cup ricotta

Directions:

1. Preheat air fryer to 360°F. Place the beaten eggs, bell pepper, oregano, salt, black pepper, and garlic and mix well. Fold in ¼ cup half of ricotta cheese.
2. Pour the egg mixture into a greased cake pan and top with the remaining ricotta. Place into the air fryer and Bake for 18-20 minutes or until the eggs are set in the center. Let the frittata cool for 5 minutes. Serve sliced.

Vegetarians Recipes

Veggie Samosas

Servings: 6
Cooking Time: 30 Minutes

Ingredients:

- 2 tbsp cream cheese, softened
- 3 tbsp minced onion
- 2 garlic cloves, minced
- 2 tbsp grated carrots
- 3 tsp olive oil
- 3 tbsp cooked green lentils
- 6 phyllo dough sheets

Directions:

1. Preheat air fryer to 390°F. Toss the onion, garlic, carrots, and some oil in a baking pan and stir. Place in the fryer and Air Fry for 2-4 minutes until the veggies are soft. Pour into a bowl. Add the lentils and cream cheese; let chill.
2. To make the dough, first lay a sheet of phyllo on a clean workspace and spritz with some olive oil, then add a second sheet on top. Repeat with the rest of the phyllo sheets until you have 3 stacks of 2 layers. Cut the stacks into 4 lengthwise strips. Add 2 tsp of the veggie mix at the bottom of each strip, then make a triangle by lifting one corner over the filling. Continue the triangle making, like folding a flag, and seal with water. Repeat until all strips are filled and folded. Bake the samosas in the air fryer for 4-7 minutes, until golden and crisp. Serve warm.

Breaded Avocado Tacos

Servings: 3
Cooking Time: 20 Minutes
Ingredients:

- 2 tomatoes, diced
- ¼ cup diced red onion
- 1 jalapeño, finely diced
- 1 tbsp lime juice
- 1 tsp lime zest
- ¼ cup chopped cilantro
- 1 tsp salt
- 1 egg
- 2 tbsp milk
- 1 cup crumbs
- ¼ cup of almond flour
- 1 avocado, sliced into fries
- 6 flour tortillas
- 1 cup coleslaw mix

Directions:

1. In a bowl, combine the tomatoes, jalapeño, red onion, lime juice, lime zest, cilantro, and salt. Let chill the pico de gallo covered in the fridge until ready to use.
2. Preheat air fryer at 375°F. In a small bowl, beat egg and milk. In another bowl, add breadcrumbs. Dip avocado slices in the egg mixture, then dredge them in the mixed almond flour and breadcrumbs. Place avocado slices in the greased frying basket and Air Fry for 5 minutes. Add 2 avocado fries to each tortilla. Top each with coleslaw mix. Serve immediately.

Hearty Salad

Servings: 2
Cooking Time: 15 Minutes
Ingredients:

- 5 oz cauliflower, cut into florets
- 2 grated carrots
- 1 tbsp olive oil
- 1 tbsp lemon juice
- 2 tbsp raisins
- 2 tbsp roasted pepitas
- 2 tbsp diced red onion
- ¼ cup mayonnaise
- 1/8 tsp black pepper
- 1 tsp cumin
- ½ tsp chia seeds
- ½ tsp sesame seeds

Directions:

1. Preheat air fryer at 350°F. Combine the cauliflower, cumin, olive oil, black pepper and lemon juice in a bowl, place it in the frying basket, and Bake for 5 minutes. Transfer it to a serving dish. Toss in the remaining ingredients. Let chill covered in the fridge until ready to use. Serve sprinkled with sesame and chia seeds.

Spiced Vegetable Galette

Servings: 4
Cooking Time: 30 Minutes
Ingredients:

- ¼ cup cooked eggplant, chopped
- ¼ cup cooked zucchini, chopped
- 1 refrigerated pie crust
- 2 eggs
- ¼ cup milk
- Salt and pepper to taste
- 1 red chili, finely sliced
- ¼ cup tomato, chopped
- ½ cup shredded mozzarella cheese

Directions:

1. Preheat air fryer to 360°F. In a baking dish, add the crust and press firmly. Trim off any excess edges. Poke a few holes. Beat the eggs in a bowl. Stir in the milk, half of the cheese, eggplant, zucchini, tomato, red chili, salt, and pepper. Mix well. Transfer the mixture to the baking dish and place in the air fryer. Bake for 15 minutes or until firm and almost crusty. Slide the basket out and top with the remaining cheese. Cook further for 5 minutes, or until golden brown. Let cool slightly and serve.

Pizza Portobello Mushrooms

Servings: 2
Cooking Time: 18 Minutes
Ingredients:

- 2 portobello mushroom caps, gills removed (see Figure 13-1)
- 1 teaspoon extra-virgin olive oil
- ¼ cup diced onion
- 1 teaspoon minced garlic
- 1 medium zucchini, shredded
- 1 teaspoon dried oregano
- ½ teaspoon black pepper
- ¼ teaspoon salt
- ⅓ cup marinara sauce
- ¼ cup shredded part-skim mozzarella cheese
- ¼ teaspoon red pepper flakes

- 2 tablespoons Parmesan cheese
- 2 tablespoons chopped basil

Directions:

1. Preheat the air fryer to 370°F.
2. Lightly spray the mushrooms with an olive oil mist and place into the air fryer to cook for 10 minutes, cap side up.
3. Add the olive oil to a pan and sauté the onion and garlic together for about 2 to 4 minutes. Stir in the zucchini, oregano, pepper, and salt, and continue to cook. When the zucchini has cooked down (usually about 4 to 6 minutes), add in the marinara sauce. Remove from the heat and stir in the mozzarella cheese.
4. Remove the mushrooms from the air fryer basket when cooking completes. Reset the temperature to 350°F.
5. Using a spoon, carefully stuff the mushrooms with the zucchini marinara mixture.
6. Return the stuffed mushrooms to the air fryer basket and cook for 5 to 8 minutes, or until the cheese is lightly browned. You should be able to easily insert a fork into the mushrooms when they're cooked.
7. Remove the mushrooms and sprinkle the red pepper flakes, Parmesan cheese, and fresh basil over the top.
8. Serve warm.

Pinto Bean Casserole

Servings: 2

Cooking Time: 15 Minutes

Ingredients:

- 1 can pinto beans
- ¼ cup tomato sauce
- 2 tbsp cornstarch
- 2 garlic cloves, minced
- ½ tsp dried oregano
- ½ tsp cumin
- 1 tsp smoked paprika
- Salt and pepper to taste

Directions:

1. Preheat air fryer to 390°F. Stir the beans, tomato sauce, cornstarch, garlic, oregano, cumin, smoked paprika, salt, and pepper in a bowl until combined. Pour the bean mix into a greased baking pan. Bake in the fryer for 4 minutes. Remove, stir, and Bake for 4 minutes or until the mix is thick and heated through. Serve hot.

Tortilla Pizza Margherita

Servings: 1

Cooking Time: 15 Minutes

Ingredients:

- 1 flour tortilla
- ¼ cup tomato sauce
- 1/3 cup grated mozzarella
- 3 basil leaves

Directions:

1. Preheat air fryer to 350°F. Put the tortilla in the greased basket and pour the sauce in the center. Spread across the whole tortilla. Sprinkle with cheese and Bake for 8-10 minutes or until crisp. Remove carefully and top with basil leaves. Serve hot.

Cheesy Eggplant Lasagna

Servings: 4

Cooking Time: 40 Minutes

Ingredients:

- ¾ cup chickpea flour
- ½ cup milk
- 3 tbsp lemon juice
- 1 tbsp chili sauce
- 2 tsp allspice
- 2 cups panko bread crumbs
- 1 eggplant, sliced
- 2 cups jarred tomato sauce
- ½ cup ricotta cheese
- 1/3 cup mozzarella cheese

Directions:

1. Preheat air fryer to 400°F. Whisk chickpea flour, milk, lemon juice, chili sauce, and allspice until smooth. Set aside. On a plate, put the breadcrumbs. Submerge each eggplant slice into the batter, shaking off any excess, and dip into the breadcrumbs until well coated. Bake for 10 minutes, turning once. Let cool slightly.
2. Spread 2 tbsp of tomato sauce at the bottom of a baking pan. Lay a single layer of eggplant slices, scatter with ricotta cheese and top with tomato sauce. Repeat the process until no ingredients are left. Scatter with mozzarella cheese on top and Bake at 350°F for 10 minutes until the eggplants are cooked and the cheese golden brown. Serve immediately.

Chili Tofu & Quinoa Bowls

Servings: 2
Cooking Time: 30 Minutes
Ingredients:

- 1 cup diced peeled sweet potatoes
- ¼ cup chopped mixed bell peppers
- 1/8 cup sprouted green lentils
- ½ onion, sliced
- 1 tsp avocado oil
- 1/8 cup chopped carrots
- 8 oz extra-firm tofu, cubed
- ½ tsp smoked paprika
- ½ tsp chili powder
- ¼ tsp salt
- 2 tsp lime zest
- 1 cup cooked quinoa
- 2 lime wedges

Directions:

1. Preheat air fryer at 350°F. Combine the onion, carrots, bell peppers, green lentils, sweet potato, and avocado oil in a bowl. In another bowl, mix the tofu, paprika, chili powder, and salt. Add veggie mixture to the frying basket and Air Fry for 8 minutes. Stir in tofu mixture and cook for 8 more minutes. Combine lime zest and quinoa. Divide into 2 serving bowls. Top each with the tofu mixture and squeeze a lime wedge over. Serve warm.

Tex-mex Stuffed Sweet Potatoes

Servings: 2
Cooking Time: 40 Minutes
Ingredients:

- 2 medium sweet potatoes
- 1 can black beans
- 2 scallions, finely sliced
- 1 tbsp hot sauce
- 1 tsp taco seasoning
- 2 tbsp lime juice
- ¼ cup Ranch dressing

Directions:

1. Preheat air fryer to 400°F. Add in sweet potatoes and Roast for 30 minutes. Toss the beans, scallions, hot sauce, taco seasoning, and lime juice. Set aside. Once the potatoes are ready, cut them lengthwise, 2/3 through. Spoon 1/4 of the bean mixture into each half and drizzle Ranch dressing before serving.

Italian Stuffed Bell Peppers

Servings: 4
Cooking Time: 75 Minutes
Ingredients:

- 4 green and red bell peppers, tops and insides discarded
- 2 russet potatoes, scrubbed and perforated with a fork
- 2 tsp olive oil
- 2 Italian sausages, cubed
- 2 tbsp milk
- 2 tbsp yogurt
- 1 tsp olive oil
- 1 tbsp Italian seasoning
- Salt and pepper to taste
- ¼ cup canned corn kernels
- ½ cup mozzarella shreds
- 2 tsp chopped parsley
- 1 cup bechamel sauce

Directions:

1. Preheat air fryer at 400°F. Rub olive oil over both potatoes and sprinkle with salt and pepper. Place them in the frying basket and Bake for 45 minutes, flipping at 30 minutes mark. Let cool onto a cutting board for 5 minutes until cool enough to handle. Scoop out cooled potato into a bowl. Discard skins.
2. Place Italian sausages in the frying basket and Air Fry for 2 minutes. Using the back of a fork, mash cooked potatoes, yogurt, milk, olive oil, Italian seasoning, salt, and pepper until smooth. Toss in cooked sausages, corn, and mozzarella cheese. Stuff bell peppers with the potato mixture. Place bell peppers in the frying basket and Bake for 10 minutes. Serve immediately sprinkled with parsley and bechamel sauce on side.

Roasted Vegetable Thai Green Curry

Servings: 4
Cooking Time: 16 Minutes
Ingredients:

- 1 (13-ounce) can coconut milk
- 3 tablespoons green curry paste
- 1 tablespoon soy sauce*
- 1 tablespoon rice wine vinegar
- 1 teaspoon sugar
- 1 teaspoon minced fresh ginger
- ½ onion, chopped
- 3 carrots, sliced
- 1 red bell pepper, chopped
- olive oil
- 10 stalks of asparagus, cut into 2-inch pieces
- 3 cups broccoli florets
- basmati rice for serving
- fresh cilantro
- crushed red pepper flakes (optional)

Directions:

1. Combine the coconut milk, green curry paste, soy sauce, rice wine vinegar, sugar and ginger in a medium saucepan and bring to a boil on the stovetop. Reduce the heat and simmer for 20 minutes while you cook the vegetables. Set aside.
2. Preheat the air fryer to 400°F.
3. Toss the onion, carrots, and red pepper together with a little olive oil and transfer the vegetables to the air fryer basket. Air-fry at 400°F for 10 minutes, shaking the basket a few times during the cooking process. Add the asparagus and broccoli florets and air-fry for an additional 6 minutes, again shaking the basket for even cooking.
4. When the vegetables are cooked to your liking, toss them with the green curry sauce and serve in bowls over basmati rice. Garnish with fresh chopped cilantro and crushed red pepper flakes.

Crunchy Rice Paper Samosas

Servings: 2
Cooking Time: 20 Minutes
Ingredients:

- 1 boiled potato, mashed
- ¼ cup green peas
- 1 tsp garam masala powder
- ½ tsp ginger garlic paste
- ½ tsp cayenne pepper
- ½ tsp turmeric powder
- Salt and pepper to taste
- 3 rice paper wrappers

Directions:

1. Preheat air fryer to 350°F. Place the mashed potatoes in a bowl. Add the peas, garam masala powder, ginger garlic paste, cayenne pepper, turmeric powder, salt, and pepper and stir until ingredients are evenly blended.
2. Lay the rice paper wrappers out on a lightly floured surface. Divide the potato mixture between the wrappers and fold the top edges over to seal. Transfer the samosas to the greased frying basket and Air Fry for 12 minutes, flipping once until the samosas are crispy and flaky. Remove and leave to cool for 5 minutes. Serve and enjoy!

Mushroom, Zucchini And Black Bean Burgers

Servings: 4
Cooking Time: 18 Minutes
Ingredients:

- 1 cup diced zucchini, (about ½ medium zucchini)
- 1 tablespoon olive oil
- salt and freshly ground black pepper
- 1 cup chopped brown mushrooms (about 3 ounces)
- 1 small clove garlic
- 1 (15-ounce) can black beans, drained and rinsed
- 1 teaspoon lemon zest
- 1 tablespoon chopped fresh cilantro
- ½ cup plain breadcrumbs
- 1 egg, beaten
- ½ teaspoon salt
- freshly ground black pepper
- whole-wheat pita bread, burger buns or brioche buns
- mayonnaise, tomato, avocado and lettuce, for serving

Directions:

1. Preheat the air fryer to 400°F.
2. Toss the zucchini with the olive oil, season with salt and freshly ground black pepper and air-fry for 6 minutes, shaking the basket once or twice while it cooks.
3. Transfer the zucchini to a food processor with the mushrooms, garlic and black beans and process until still a little chunky but broken down and pasty. Transfer the mixture to a bowl. Add the lemon zest, cilantro, breadcrumbs and egg and mix well. Season

again with salt and freshly ground black pepper. Shape the mixture into four burger patties and refrigerate for at least 15 minutes.

4. Preheat the air fryer to 370°F. Transfer two of the veggie burgers to the air fryer basket and air-fry for 12 minutes, flipping the burgers gently halfway through the cooking time. Keep the burgers warm by loosely tenting them with foil while you cook the remaining two burgers. Return the first batch of burgers back into the air fryer with the second batch for the last two minutes of cooking to re-heat.

5. Serve on toasted whole-wheat pita bread, burger buns or brioche buns with some mayonnaise, tomato, avocado and lettuce.

General Tso's Cauliflower

Servings: 4
Cooking Time: 15 Minutes

Ingredients:

- 1 head cauliflower cut into florets
- ¾ cup all-purpose flour, divided*
- 3 eggs, lightly beaten
- 1 cup panko breadcrumbs*
- canola or peanut oil, in a spray bottle
- 2 tablespoons oyster sauce
- ¼ cup soy sauce
- 2 teaspoons chili paste
- 2 tablespoons rice wine vinegar
- 2 tablespoons sugar
- ¼ cup water
- white or brown rice for serving
- steamed broccoli

Directions:

1. Set up dredging station using three bowls. Place the cauliflower in a large bowl and sprinkle ¼ cup of the flour over the top. Place the eggs in a second bowl and combine the panko breadcrumbs and remaining ½ cup flour in a third bowl. Toss the cauliflower in the flour to coat all the florets thoroughly. Dip the cauliflower florets in the eggs and finally toss them in the breadcrumbs to coat on all sides. Place the coated cauliflower florets on a baking sheet and spray generously with canola or peanut oil.
2. Preheat the air fryer to 400°F.
3. Air-fry the cauliflower at 400°F for 15 minutes, flipping the florets over for the last 3 minutes of the cooking process and spraying again with oil.
4. While the cauliflower is air-frying, make the General Tso Sauce. Combine the oyster sauce, soy sauce, chili paste, rice wine vinegar, sugar and water in a saucepan and bring the mixture to a boil on the stove top. Lower the heat and let it simmer for 10 minutes, stirring occasionally.
5. When the timer is up on the air fryer, transfer the cauliflower to a large bowl, pour the sauce over it all and toss to coat. Serve with white or brown rice and some steamed broccoli.

Veggie Fried Rice

Servings: 4
Cooking Time: 25 Minutes

Ingredients:

- 1 cup cooked brown rice
- ⅓ cup chopped onion
- ½ cup chopped carrots
- ½ cup chopped bell peppers
- ½ cup chopped broccoli florets
- 3 tablespoons low-sodium soy sauce
- 1 tablespoon sesame oil
- 1 teaspoon ground ginger
- 1 teaspoon ground garlic powder
- ½ teaspoon black pepper
- ⅛ teaspoon salt
- 2 large eggs

Directions:

1. Preheat the air fryer to 370°F.
2. In a large bowl, mix together the brown rice, onions, carrots, bell pepper, and broccoli.
3. In a small bowl, whisk together the soy sauce, sesame oil, ginger, garlic powder, pepper, salt, and eggs.
4. Pour the egg mixture into the rice and vegetable mixture and mix together.
5. Liberally spray a 7-inch springform pan (or compatible air fryer dish) with olive oil. Add the rice mixture to the pan and cover with aluminum foil.
6. Place a metal trivet into the air fryer basket and set the pan on top. Cook for 15 minutes. Carefully remove the pan from basket, discard the foil, and mix the rice. Return the rice to the air fryer basket, turning down the temperature to 350°F and cooking another 10 minutes.
7. Remove and let cool 5 minutes. Serve warm.

Cheese Ravioli

Servings: 4
Cooking Time: 9 Minutes
Ingredients:

- 1 egg
- 1/4 cup milk
- 1 cup breadcrumbs
- 2 teaspoons Italian seasoning
- 1/8 teaspoon ground rosemary
- 1/4 teaspoon basil
- 1/4 teaspoon parsley
- 9-ounce package uncooked cheese ravioli
- 1/4 cup flour
- oil for misting or cooking spray

Directions:

1. Preheat air fryer to 390°F.
2. In a medium bowl, beat together egg and milk.
3. In a large plastic bag, mix together the breadcrumbs, Italian seasoning, rosemary, basil, and parsley.
4. Place all the ravioli and the flour in a bag or a bowl with a lid and shake to coat.
5. Working with a handful at a time, drop floured ravioli into egg wash. Remove ravioli, letting excess drip off, and place in bag with breadcrumbs.
6. When all ravioli are in the breadcrumbs' bag, shake well to coat all pieces.
7. Dump enough ravioli into air fryer basket to form one layer. Mist with oil or cooking spray. Dump the remaining ravioli on top of the first layer and mist with oil.
8. Cook for 5minutes. Shake well and spray with oil. Break apart any ravioli stuck together and spray any spots you missed the first time.
9. Cook 4 minutes longer, until ravioli puff up and are crispy golden brown.

Curried Potato, Cauliflower And Pea Turnovers

Servings: 4
Cooking Time: 40 Minutes
Ingredients:

- Dough:
- 2 cups all-purpose flour
- 1/2 teaspoon baking powder
- 1 teaspoon salt
- freshly ground black pepper
- 1/4 teaspoon dried thyme
- 1/4 cup canola oil
- 1/2 to 2/3 cup water
- Turnover Filling:
- 1 tablespoon canola or vegetable oil
- 1 onion, finely chopped
- 1 clove garlic, minced
- 1 tablespoon grated fresh ginger
- 1/2 teaspoon cumin seeds
- 1/2 teaspoon fennel seeds
- 1 teaspoon curry powder
- 2 russet potatoes, diced
- 2 cups cauliflower florets
- 1/2 cup frozen peas
- 2 tablespoons chopped fresh cilantro
- salt and freshly ground black pepper
- 2 tablespoons butter, melted
- mango chutney, for serving

Directions:

1. Start by making the dough. Combine the flour, baking powder, salt, pepper and dried thyme in a mixing bowl or the bowl of a stand mixer. Drizzle in the canola oil and pinch it together with your fingers to turn the flour into a crumby mixture. Stir in the water (enough to bring the dough together). Knead the dough for 5 minutes or so until it is smooth. Add a little more water or flour as needed. Let the dough rest while you make the turnover filling.
2. Preheat a large skillet on the stovetop over medium-high heat. Add the oil and sauté the onion until it starts to become tender – about 4 minutes. Add the garlic and ginger and continue to cook for another minute. Add the dried spices and toss everything to coat. Add the potatoes and cauliflower to the skillet and pour in 1½ cups of water. Simmer everything together for 20 to 25 minutes, or until the potatoes are soft and most of the water has evaporated. If the water has evaporated and the vegetables still need more time, just add a little water and continue to simmer until everything is tender. Stir well, crushing the potatoes and cauliflower a little as you do so. Stir in the peas and cilantro, season to taste with salt and freshly ground black pepper and set aside to cool.
3. Divide the dough into 4 balls. Roll the dough balls out into 1/4-inch thick circles. Divide the cooled potato filling between the dough circles, placing a mound of the filling on one side of each piece of dough, leaving an empty border around the edge of the dough. Brush the edges of the dough with a little water and fold one edge of circle over the filling to meet the other edge of

the circle, creating a half moon. Pinch the edges together with your fingers and then press the edge with the tines of a fork to decorate and seal.

4. Preheat the air fryer to 380°F.

5. Spray or brush the air fryer basket with oil. Brush the turnovers with the melted butter and place 2 turnovers into the air fryer basket. Air-fry for 15 minutes. Flip the turnovers over and air-fry for another 5 minutes. Repeat with the remaining 2 turnovers.

6. These will be very hot when they come out of the air fryer. Let them cool for at least 20 minutes before serving warm with mango chutney.

Pineapple & Veggie Souvlaki

Servings: 4

Cooking Time: 35 Minutes

Ingredients:

- 1 can pineapple rings in pineapple juice
- 1 red bell pepper, stemmed and seeded
- 1/3 cup butter
- 2 tbsp apple cider vinegar
- 2 tbsp hot sauce
- 1 tbsp allspice
- 1 tsp ground nutmeg
- 16 oz feta cheese
- 1 red onion, peeled
- 8 mushrooms, quartered

Directions:

1. Preheat air fryer to 400°F. Whisk the butter, pineapple juice, apple vinegar, hot sauce, allspice, and nutmeg until smooth. Set aside. Slice feta cheese into 16 cubes, then the bell pepper into 16 chunks, and finally red onion into 8 wedges, separating each wedge into 2 pieces.

2. Cut pineapple ring into quarters. Place veggie cubes and feta into the butter bowl and toss to coat. Thread the veggies, tofu, and pineapple onto 8 skewers, alternating 16 pieces on each skewer. Grill for 15 minutes until golden brown and cooked. Serve warm.

Green Bean Sautée

Servings: 4

Cooking Time: 25 Minutes

Ingredients:

- 1 ½ lb green beans, trimmed
- 1 tbsp olive oil
- ½ tsp garlic powder
- Salt and pepper to taste
- 4 garlic cloves, thinly sliced
- 1 tbsp fresh basil, chopped

Directions:

1. Preheat the air fryer to 375°F. Toss the beans with the olive oil, garlic powder, salt, and pepper in a bowl, then add to the frying basket. Air Fry for 6 minutes, shaking the basket halfway through the cooking time. Add garlic to the air fryer and cook for 3-6 minutes or until the green beans are tender and the garlic slices start to brown. Sprinkle with basil and serve warm.

Fennel Tofu Bites

Servings: 4

Cooking Time: 35 Minutes

Ingredients:

- 1/3 cup vegetable broth
- 2 tbsp tomato sauce
- 2 tsp soy sauce
- 1 tbsp nutritional yeast
- 1 tsp Italian seasoning
- 1 tsp granulated sugar
- 1 tsp ginger grated
- ½ tsp fennel seeds
- ½ tsp garlic powder
- Salt and pepper to taste
- 14 oz firm tofu, cubed
- 2/3 cup bread crumbs
- 1 tsp Italian seasoning
- 2 tsp toasted sesame seeds
- 1 cup marinara sauce, warm

Directions:

1. In a large bowl, whisk the vegetable broth, soy sauce, ginger, tomato sauce, nutritional yeast, Italian seasoning, sugar, fennel seeds, garlic powder, salt and black pepper. Toss in tofu to coat. Let marinate covered in the fridge for 30 minutes, tossing once.

2. Preheat air fryer at 350°F. Mix the breadcrumbs, Italian seasoning, and salt in a bowl. Strain marinade from tofu cubes and dredge them in the breadcrumb mixture. Place tofu cubes in the greased frying basket and Air Fry for 10 minutes, turning once. Serve sprinkled with sesame seeds and marinara sauce on the side.

Home-style Cinnamon Rolls

Servings: 4
Cooking Time: 40 Minutes

Ingredients:

- ½ pizza dough
- 1/3 cup dark brown sugar
- ¼ cup butter, softened
- ½ tsp ground cinnamon

Directions:

1. Preheat air fryer to 360°F. Roll out the dough into a rectangle. Using a knife, spread the brown sugar and butter, covering all the edges, and sprinkle with cinnamon.Fold the long side of the dough into a log, then cut it into 8 equal pieces, avoiding compression. Place the rolls, spiral-side up, onto a parchment-lined sheet. Let rise for 20 minutes. Grease the rolls with cooking spray and Bake for 8 minutes until golden brown. Serve right away.

Quick-to-make Quesadillas

Servings: 4
Cooking Time: 30 Minutes

Ingredients:

- 12 oz goat cheese
- 2 tbsp vinegar
- 1 tbsp Taco seasoning
- 1 ripe avocado, pitted
- 4 scallions, finely sliced
- 2 tbsp lemon juice
- 4 flour tortillas
- ¼ cup hot sauce
- ½ cup Alfredo sauce
- 16 cherry tomatoes, halved

Directions:

1. Preheat air fryer to 400°F. Slice goat cheese into 4 pieces. Set aside. In a bowl, whisk vinegar and taco seasoning until combined. Submerge each slice into the vinegar and Air Fry for 12 minutes until crisp, turning once. Let cool slightly before cutting into 1/2-inch thick strips.
2. Using a fork, mash the avocado in a bowl. Stir in scallions and lemon juice and set aside. Lay one tortilla on a flat surface, cut from one edge to the center, then spread ¼ of the avocado mixture on one quadrant, 1 tbsp of hot sauce on the next quadrant, and finally 2 tbsp of Alfredo sauce on the other half. Top the non-sauce half with ¼ of cherry tomatoes and ¼ of goat cheese strips.
3. To fold, start with the avocado quadrant, folding each over the next one until you create a stacked triangle. Repeat the process with the remaining tortillas. Air Fry for 5 minutes until crispy, turning once. Serve warm.

Cheesy Enchilada Stuffed Baked Potatoes

Servings: 4
Cooking Time: 37 Minutes

Ingredients:

- 2 medium russet potatoes, washed
- One 15-ounce can mild red enchilada sauce
- One 15-ounce can low-sodium black beans, rinsed and drained
- 1 teaspoon taco seasoning
- ½ cup shredded cheddar cheese
- 1 medium avocado, halved
- ½ teaspoon garlic powder
- ¼ teaspoon black pepper
- ¼ teaspoon salt
- 2 teaspoons fresh lime juice
- 2 tablespoon chopped red onion
- ¼ cup chopped cilantro

Directions:

1. Preheat the air fryer to 390°F.
2. Puncture the outer surface of the potatoes with a fork.
3. Set the potatoes inside the air fryer basket and cook for 20 minutes, rotate, and cook another 10 minutes.
4. In a large bowl, mix the enchilada sauce, black beans, and taco seasoning.
5. When the potatoes have finished cooking, carefully remove them from the air fryer basket and let cool for 5 minutes.
6. Using a pair of tongs to hold the potato if it's still too hot to touch, slice the potato in half lengthwise. Use a spoon to scoop out the potato flesh and add it into the bowl with the enchilada sauce. Mash the potatoes with the enchilada sauce mixture, creating a uniform stuffing.
7. Place the potato skins into an air-fryer-safe pan and stuff the halves with the enchilada stuffing. Sprinkle the cheese over the top of each potato.
8. Set the air fryer temperature to 350°F, return the pan to the air fryer basket, and cook for another 5 to 7 minutes to heat the potatoes and melt the cheese.

9. While the potatoes are cooking, take the avocado and scoop out the flesh into a small bowl. Mash it with the back of a fork; then mix in the garlic powder, pepper, salt, lime juice, and onion. Set aside.

10. When the potatoes have finished cooking, remove the pan from the air fryer and place the potato halves on a plate. Top with avocado mash and fresh cilantro. Serve immediately.

Caprese-style Sandwiches

Servings: 2

Cooking Time: 20 Minutes

Ingredients:

- 2 tbsp balsamic vinegar
- 4 sandwich bread slices
- 2 oz mozzarella shreds
- 3 tbsp pesto sauce
- 2 tomatoes, sliced
- 8 basil leaves
- 8 baby spinach leaves
- 2 tbsp olive oil

Directions:

1. Preheat air fryer at 350°F. Drizzle balsamic vinegar on the bottom of bread slices and smear with pesto sauce. Then, layer mozzarella cheese, tomatoes, baby spinach leaves and basil leaves on top. Add top bread slices. Rub the outside top and bottom of each sandwich with olive oil. Place them in the frying basket and Bake for 5 minutes, flipping once. Serve right away.

Smoky Sweet Potato Fries

Servings: 4

Cooking Time: 25 Minutes

Ingredients:

- 2 large sweet potatoes, peeled and sliced
- 1 tbsp olive oil
- Salt and pepper to taste
- 1/4 tsp garlic powder
- 1/4 tsp smoked paprika
- 1 tbsp pumpkin pie spice
- 1 tbsp chopped parsley

Directions:

1. Preheat air fryer to 375°F. Toss sweet potato slices, olive oil, salt, pepper, garlic powder, pumpkin pie spice and paprika in a large bowl. Arrange the potatoes in a single layer in the frying basket. Air Fry for 5 minutes, then shake the basket. Air Fry for another 5 minutes and shake the basket again. Air Fry for 2-5 minutes until crispy. Serve sprinkled with parsley and enjoy.

Mexican Twice Air-fried Sweet Potatoes

Servings: 2

Cooking Time: 42 Minutes

Ingredients:

- 2 large sweet potatoes
- olive oil
- salt and freshly ground black pepper
- ⅓ cup diced red onion
- ⅓ cup diced red bell pepper
- 1/2 cup canned black beans, drained and rinsed
- 1/2 cup corn kernels, fresh or frozen
- 1/2 teaspoon chili powder
- 1 1/2 cups grated pepper jack cheese, divided
- Jalapeño peppers, sliced

Directions:

1. Preheat the air fryer to 400°F.
2. Rub the outside of the sweet potatoes with olive oil and season with salt and freshly ground black pepper. Transfer the potatoes into the air fryer basket and air-fry at 400°F for 30 minutes, rotating the potatoes a few times during the cooking process.
3. While the potatoes are air-frying, start the potato filling. Preheat a large sauté pan over medium heat on the stovetop. Add the onion and pepper and sauté for a few minutes, until the vegetables start to soften. Add the black beans, corn, and chili powder and sauté for another 3 minutes. Set the mixture aside.
4. Remove the sweet potatoes from the air fryer and let them rest for 5 minutes. Slice off one inch of the flattest side of both potatoes. Scrape the potato flesh out of the potatoes, leaving half an inch of potato flesh around the edge of the potato. Place all the potato flesh into a large bowl and mash it with a fork. Add the black bean mixture and 1 cup of the pepper jack cheese to the mashed sweet potatoes. Season with salt and freshly ground black pepper and mix well. Stuff the hollowed out potato shells with the black bean and sweet potato mixture, mounding the filling high in the potatoes.
5. Transfer the stuffed potatoes back into the air fryer basket and air-fry at 370°F for 10 minutes. Sprinkle the remaining cheese on top of each stuffed potato, lower the heat to 340°F and air-fry for an additional 2 minutes to melt the cheese. Top with a couple slices of Jalapeño pepper and serve warm with a green salad.

Sushi-style Deviled Eggs

Servings:4
Cooking Time: 20 Minutes
Ingredients:

- ¼ cup crabmeat, shells discarded
- 4 eggs
- 2 tbsp mayonnaise
- ½ tsp soy sauce
- ¼ avocado, diced
- ¼ tsp wasabi powder
- 2 tbsp diced cucumber
- 1 sheet nori, sliced
- 8 jarred pickled ginger slices
- 1 tsp toasted sesame seeds
- 2 spring onions, sliced

Directions:

1. Preheat air fryer to 260°F. Place the eggs in muffin cups to avoid bumping around and cracking during the cooking process. Add silicone cups to the frying basket and Air Fry for 15 minutes. Remove and plunge the eggs immediately into an ice bath to cool, about 5 minutes. Carefully peel and slice them in half lengthwise. Spoon yolks into a separate medium bowl and arrange white halves on a large plate. Mash the yolks with a fork. Stir in mayonnaise, soy sauce, avocado, and wasabi powder until smooth. Mix in cucumber and spoon into white halves. Scatter eggs with crabmeat, nori, pickled ginger, spring onions and sesame seeds to serve.

Asparagus, Mushroom And Cheese Soufflés

Servings: 3
Cooking Time: 21 Minutes
Ingredients:

- butter
- grated Parmesan cheese
- 3 button mushrooms, thinly sliced
- 8 spears asparagus, sliced ½-inch long
- 1 teaspoon olive oil
- 1 tablespoon butter
- 4½ teaspoons flour
- pinch paprika
- pinch ground nutmeg
- salt and freshly ground black pepper
- ½ cup milk
- ½ cup grated Gruyère cheese or other Swiss cheese (about 2 ounces)
- 2 eggs, separated

Directions:

1. Butter three 6-ounce ramekins and dust with grated Parmesan cheese. (Butter the ramekins and then coat the butter with Parmesan by shaking it around in the ramekin and dumping out any excess.)
2. Preheat the air fryer to 400°F.
3. Toss the mushrooms and asparagus in a bowl with the olive oil. Transfer the vegetables to the air fryer and air-fry for 7 minutes, shaking the basket once or twice to redistribute the Ingredients while they cook.
4. While the vegetables are cooking, make the soufflé base. Melt the butter in a saucepan on the stovetop over medium heat. Add the flour, stir and cook for a minute or two. Add the paprika, nutmeg, salt and pepper. Whisk in the milk and bring the mixture to a simmer to thicken. Remove the pan from the heat and add the cheese, stirring to melt. Let the mixture cool for just a few minutes and then whisk the egg yolks in, one at a time. Stir in the cooked mushrooms and asparagus. Let this soufflé base cool.
5. In a separate bowl, whisk the egg whites to soft peak stage (the point at which the whites can almost stand up on the end of your whisk). Fold the whipped egg whites into the soufflé base, adding a little at a time.
6. Preheat the air fryer to 330°F.
7. Transfer the batter carefully to the buttered ramekins, leaving about ½-inch at the top. Place the ramekins into the air fryer basket and air-fry for 14 minutes. The soufflés should have risen nicely and be brown on top. Serve immediately.

Corn And Pepper Jack Chile Rellenos With Roasted Tomato Sauce

Servings: 3
Cooking Time: 30 Minutes
Ingredients:

- 3 Poblano peppers
- 1 cup all-purpose flour*
- salt and freshly ground black pepper
- 2 eggs, lightly beaten
- 1 cup plain breadcrumbs*
- olive oil, in a spray bottle
- Sauce
- 2 cups cherry tomatoes
- 1 Jalapeño pepper, halved and seeded
- 1 clove garlic
- ¼ red onion, broken into large pieces

- 1 tablespoon olive oil
- salt, to taste
- 2 tablespoons chopped fresh cilantro
- Filling
- olive oil
- ¼ red onion, finely chopped
- 1 teaspoon minced garlic
- 1 cup corn kernels, fresh or frozen
- 2 cups grated pepper jack cheese

Directions:

1. Start by roasting the peppers. Preheat the air fryer to 400°F. Place the peppers into the air fryer basket and air-fry at 400°F for 10 minutes, turning them over halfway through the cooking time. Remove the peppers from the basket and cover loosely with foil.
2. While the peppers are cooling, make the roasted tomato sauce. Place all sauce Ingredients except for the cilantro into the air fryer basket and air-fry at 400°F for 10 minutes, shaking the basket once or twice. When the sauce Ingredients have finished air-frying, transfer everything to a blender or food processor and blend or process to a smooth sauce, adding a little warm water to get the desired consistency. Season to taste with salt, add the cilantro and set aside.
3. While the sauce Ingredients are cooking in the air fryer, make the filling. Heat a skillet on the stovetop over medium heat. Add the olive oil and sauté the red onion and garlic for 4 to 5 minutes. Transfer the onion and garlic to a bowl, stir in the corn and cheese, and set aside.
4. Set up a dredging station with three shallow dishes. Place the flour, seasoned with salt and pepper, in the first shallow dish. Place the eggs in the second dish, and fill the third shallow dish with the breadcrumbs. When the peppers have cooled, carefully slice into one side of the pepper to create an opening. Pull the seeds out of the peppers and peel away the skins, trying not to tear the pepper. Fill each pepper with some of the corn and cheese filling and close the pepper up again by folding one side of the opening over the other. Carefully roll each pepper in the seasoned flour, then into the egg and finally into the breadcrumbs to coat on all sides, trying not to let the pepper fall open. Spray the peppers on all sides with a little olive oil.
5. Air-fry two peppers at a time at 350°F for 6 minutes. Turn the peppers over and air-fry for another 4 minutes. Serve the peppers warm on a bed of the roasted tomato sauce.

Vegan Buddha Bowls(1)

Servings: 2
Cooking Time: 45 Minutes

Ingredients:

- ½ cup quinoa
- 1 cup sweet potato cubes
- 12 oz broccoli florets
- ¾ cup bread crumbs
- ¼ cup chickpea flour
- ¼ cup hot sauce
- 16 oz super-firm tofu, cubed
- 1 tsp lemon juice
- 2 tsp olive oil
- Salt to taste
- 2 scallions, thinly sliced
- 1 tbsp sesame seeds

Directions:

1. Preheat air fryer to 400°F. Add quinoa and 1 cup of boiling water in a baking pan, cover it with aluminum foil, and Air Fry for 10 minutes. Set aside covered. Put the sweet potatoes in the basket and Air Fry for 2 minutes. Add in broccoli and Air Fry for 5 more minutes. Shake up and cook for another 3 minutes. Set the veggies aside.
2. On a plate, put the breadcrumbs. In a bowl, whisk chickpea flour and hot sauce. Toss in tofu cubes until coated and dip them in the breadcrumbs. Air Fry for 10 minutes until crispy. Share quinoa and fried veggies into 2 bowls. Top with crispy tofu and drizzle with lemon juice, olive oil and salt to taste. Scatter with scallions and sesame seeds before serving.

Roasted Vegetable Pita Pizza

Servings: 4
Cooking Time: 20 Minutes

Ingredients:

- 1 medium red bell pepper, seeded and cut into quarters
- 1 teaspoon extra-virgin olive oil
- ⅛ teaspoon black pepper
- ⅛ teaspoon salt
- Two 6-inch whole-grain pita breads
- 6 tablespoons pesto sauce
- ¼ small red onion, thinly sliced
- ½ cup shredded part-skim mozzarella cheese

Directions:

1. Preheat the air fryer to 400°F.

2. In a small bowl, toss the bell peppers with the olive oil, pepper, and salt.
3. Place the bell peppers in the air fryer and cook for 15 minutes, shaking every 5 minutes to prevent burning.
4. Remove the peppers and set aside. Turn the air fryer temperature down to 350°F.
5. Lay the pita bread on a flat surface. Cover each with half the pesto sauce; then top with even portions of the red bell peppers and onions. Sprinkle cheese over the top. Spray the air fryer basket with olive oil mist.
6. Carefully lift the pita bread into the air fryer basket with a spatula.
7. Cook for 5 to 8 minutes, or until the outer edges begin to brown and the cheese is melted.
8. Serve warm with desired sides.

Vegetarian Paella

Servings: 3
Cooking Time: 50 Minutes

Ingredients:

- ½ cup chopped artichoke hearts
- ½ sliced red bell peppers
- 4 mushrooms, thinly sliced
- ½ cup canned diced tomatoes
- ½ cup canned chickpeas
- 3 tbsp hot sauce
- 2 tbsp lemon juice
- 1 tbsp allspice
- 1 cup rice

Directions:

1. Preheat air fryer to 400°F. Combine the artichokes, peppers, mushrooms, tomatoes and their juices, chickpeas, hot sauce, lemon juice, and allspice in a baking pan. Roast for 10 minutes. Pour in rice and 2 cups of boiling water, cover with aluminum foil, and Roast for 22 minutes. Discard the foil and Roast for 3 minutes until the top is crisp. Let cool slightly before stirring. Serve.

Italian-style Fried Cauliflower

Servings: 4
Cooking Time: 35 Minutes

Ingredients:

- 2 eggs
- 1/3 cup all-purpose flour
- ½ tsp Italian seasoning
- ½ cup bread crumbs
- 1 tsp garlic powder
- 3 tsp grated Parmesan cheese
- Salt and pepper to taste
- 1 head cauliflower, cut into florets
- ½ tsp ground coriander

Directions:

1. Preheat air fryer to 370°F. Set out 3 small bowls. In the first, mix the flour with Italian seasoning. In the second, beat the eggs. In the third bowl, combine the crumbs, garlic, Parmesan, ground coriander, salt, and pepper.
2. Dip the cauliflower in the flour, then dredge in egg, and finally in the bread crumb mixture. Place a batch of cauliflower in the greased frying basket and spray with cooking oil. Bake for 10-12 minutes, shaking once until golden. Serve warm and enjoy!

Chive Potato Pierogi

Servings: 4
Cooking Time: 55 Minutes

Ingredients:

- 2 boiled potatoes, mashed
- Salt and pepper to taste
- 1 tsp cumin powder
- 2 tbsp sour cream
- ¼ cup grated Parmesan
- 2 tbsp chopped chives
- 1 tbsp chopped parsley
- 1 ¼ cups flour
- ¼ tsp garlic powder
- ¾ cup Greek yogurt
- 1 egg

Directions:

1. Combine the mashed potatoes along with sour cream, cumin, parsley, chives, pepper, and salt and stir until slightly chunky. Mix the flour, salt, and garlic powder in a large bowl. Stir in yogurt until it comes together as a sticky dough. Knead in the bowl for about 2-3 minutes to make it smooth. Whisk the egg and 1 teaspoon of water in a small bowl. Roll out the dough on a lightly floured work surface to ¼-inch thickness. Cut out 12 circles with a cookie cutter.
2. Preheat air fryer to 350°F. Divide the potato mixture and Parmesan cheese between the dough circles. Brush the edges of them with the egg wash and fold the dough over the filling into half-moon shapes. Crimp the edges with a fork to seal. Arrange the on the greased frying basket and Air Fry for 8-10 minutes, turning the pierogies once, until the outside is golden. Serve warm.

Easy Zucchini Lasagna Roll-ups

Servings: 2
Cooking Time: 40 Minutes
Ingredients:

- 2 medium zucchini
- 2 tbsp lemon juice
- 1 ½ cups ricotta cheese
- 1 tbsp allspice
- 2 cups marinara sauce
- 1/3 cup mozzarella cheese

Directions:

1. Preheat air fryer to 400°F. Cut the ends of each zucchini, then slice into 1/4-inch thick pieces and drizzle with lemon juice. Roast for 5 minutes until slightly tender. Let cool slightly. Combine ricotta cheese and allspice in a bowl; set aside. Spread 2 tbsp of marinara sauce on the bottom of a baking pan. Spoon 1-2 tbsp of the ricotta mixture onto each slice, roll up each slice and place them spiral-side up in the pan. Scatter with the remaining ricotta mixture and drizzle with marinara sauce. Top with mozzarella cheese and Bake at 360°F for 20 minutes until the cheese is bubbly and golden brown. Serve warm.

Sesame Orange Tofu With Snow Peas

Servings: 4
Cooking Time: 40 Minutes
Ingredients:

- 14 oz tofu, cubed
- 1 tbsp tamari
- 1 tsp olive oil
- 1 tsp sesame oil
- 1 ½ tbsp cornstarch, divided
- ½ tsp salt
- ¼ tsp garlic powder
- 1 cup snow peas
- ½ cup orange juice
- ¼ cup vegetable broth
- 1 orange, zested
- 1 garlic clove, minced
- ¼ tsp ground ginger
- 2 scallions, chopped
- 1 tbsp sesame seeds
- 2 cups cooked jasmine rice
- 2 tbsp chopped parsley

Directions:

1. Preheat air fryer to 400°F. Combine tofu, tamari, olive oil, and sesame oil in a large bowl until tofu is coated. Add in 1 tablespoon cornstarch, salt, and garlic powder and toss. Arrange the tofu on the frying basket. Air Fry for 5 minutes, then shake the basket. Add snow peas and Air Fry for 5 minutes. Place tofu mixture in a bowl.
2. Bring the orange juice, vegetable broth, orange zest, garlic, and ginger to a boil over medium heat in a small saucepan. Whisk the rest of the cornstarch and 1 tablespoon water in a small bowl to make a slurry. Pour the slurry into the saucepan and constantly stir for 2 minutes until the sauce has thickened. Let off the heat for 2 minutes. Pour the orange sauce, scallions, and sesame seeds in the bowl with the tofu and stir to coat. Serve with jasmine rice sprinkled with parsley. Enjoy!

Thai Peanut Veggie Burgers

Servings: 6
Cooking Time: 14 Minutes
Ingredients:

- One 15.5-ounce can cannellini beans
- 1 teaspoon minced garlic
- ¼ cup chopped onion
- 1 Thai chili pepper, sliced
- 2 tablespoons natural peanut butter
- ½ teaspoon black pepper
- ½ teaspoon salt
- ⅓ cup all-purpose flour (optional)
- ½ cup cooked quinoa
- 1 large carrot, grated
- 1 cup shredded red cabbage
- ¼ cup peanut dressing
- ¼ cup chopped cilantro
- 6 Hawaiian rolls
- 6 butterleaf lettuce leaves

Directions:

1. Preheat the air fryer to 350°F.
2. To a blender or food processor fitted with a metal blade, add the beans, garlic, onion, chili pepper, peanut butter, pepper, and salt. Pulse for 5 to 10 seconds. Do not over process. The mixture should be coarse, not smooth.
3. Remove from the blender or food processor and spoon into a large bowl. Mix in the cooked quinoa and carrots. At this point, the mixture should begin to hold together to form small patties. If the dough appears to

be too sticky (meaning you likely processed a little too long), add the flour to hold the patties together.

4. Using a large spoon, form 8 equal patties out of the batter.

5. Liberally spray a metal trivet with olive oil spray and set in the air fryer basket. Place the patties into the basket, leaving enough space to be able to turn them with a spatula.

6. Cook for 7 minutes, flip, and cook another 7 minutes.

7. Remove from the heat and repeat with additional patties.

8. To serve, place the red cabbage in a bowl and toss with peanut dressing and cilantro. Place the veggie burger on a bun, and top with a slice of lettuce and cabbage slaw.

Tomato & Squash Stuffed Mushrooms

Servings:2

Cooking Time: 15 Minutes

Ingredients:

- 12 whole white button mushrooms
- 3 tsp olive oil
- 2 tbsp diced zucchini
- 1 tsp soy sauce
- 1/4 tsp salt
- 2 tbsp tomato paste
- 1 tbsp chopped parsley

Directions:

1. Preheat air fryer to 350°F. Remove the stems from the mushrooms. Chop the stems finely and set in a bowl. Brush 1 tsp of olive oil around the top ridge of mushroom caps. To the bowl of the stem, add all ingredients, except for parsley, and mix. Divide and press mixture into tops of mushroom caps. Place the mushrooms in the frying basket and Air Fry for 5 minutes. Top with parsley. Serve.

Creamy Broccoli & Mushroom Casserole

Servings:4

Cooking Time: 30 Minutes

Ingredients:

- 4 cups broccoli florets, chopped
- 1 cup crushed cheddar cheese crisps
- 1/4 cup diced onion
- 1/4 tsp dried thyme
- 1/4 tsp dried marjoram
- 1/4 tsp dried oregano
- 1/2 cup diced mushrooms
- 1 egg
- 2 tbsp sour cream
- 1/4 cup mayonnaise
- Salt and pepper to taste

Directions:

1. Preheat air fryer to 350°F. Combine all ingredients, except for the cheese crisps, in a bowl. Spoon mixture into a round cake pan. Place cake pan in the frying basket and Bake for 14 minutes. Let sit for 10 minutes. Distribute crushed cheddar cheese crisps over the top and serve.

Vegetable Side Dishes Recipes

Salt And Pepper Baked Potatoes

Cooking Time: 40 Minutes
Servings: 4

Ingredients:

- 1 to 2 tablespoons olive oil
- 4 medium russet potatoes (about 9 to 10 ounces each)
- salt and coarsely ground black pepper
- butter, sour cream, chopped fresh chives, scallions or bacon bits (optional)

Directions:

1. Preheat the air fryer to 400°F.
2. Rub the olive oil all over the potatoes and season them generously with salt and coarsely ground black pepper. Pierce all sides of the potatoes several times with the tines of a fork.
3. Air-fry for 40 minutes, turning the potatoes over halfway through the cooking time.
4. Serve the potatoes, split open with butter, sour cream, fresh chives, scallions or bacon bits.

Panko-crusted Zucchini Fries

Servings: 6
Cooking Time: 8 Minutes

Ingredients:

- 3 medium zucchinis
- ½ cup flour
- 1 teaspoon salt, divided
- ½ teaspoon black pepper, divided
- ¾ teaspoon dried thyme, divided
- 2 large eggs
- 1 ½ cups whole-wheat or plain panko breadcrumbs
- ½ cup grated Parmesan cheese

Directions:

1. Preheat the air fryer to 380°F.
2. Slice the zucchinis in half lengthwise, then into long strips about ½-inch thick, like thick fries.
3. In a medium bowl, mix the flour, ½ teaspoon of the salt, ¼ teaspoon of the black pepper, and ½ teaspoon of thyme.
4. In a separate bowl, whisk together the eggs, ½ teaspoon of the salt, and ¼ teaspoon of the black pepper.
5. In a third bowl, combine the breadcrumbs, cheese, and the remaining ¼ teaspoon of dried thyme.
6. Working with one zucchini fry at a time, dip the zucchini fry first into the flour mixture, then into the whisked eggs, and finally into the breading. Repeat until all the fries are breaded.
7. Place the zucchini fries into the air fryer basket, spray with cooking spray, and cook for 4 minutes; shake the basket and cook another 4 to 6 minutes or until golden brown and crispy.
8. Remove and serve warm.

Steakhouse Baked Potatoes

Servings: 3
Cooking Time: 55 Minutes

Ingredients:

- 3 10-ounce russet potatoes
- 2 tablespoons Olive oil
- 1 teaspoon Table salt

Directions:

1. Preheat the air fryer to 375°F .
2. Poke holes all over each potato with a fork. Rub the skin of each potato with 2 teaspoons of the olive oil, then sprinkle ¼ teaspoon salt all over each potato.
3. When the machine is at temperature, set the potatoes in the basket in one layer with as much air space between them as possible. Air-fry for 50 minutes, turning once, or until soft to the touch but with crunchy skins. If the machine is at 360°F, you may need to add up to 5 minutes to the cooking time.
4. Use kitchen tongs to gently transfer the baked potatoes to a wire rack. Cool for 5 or 10 minutes before serving.

Steak Fries

Cooking Time: 20 Minutes
Servings: 4

Ingredients:

- 2 russet potatoes, scrubbed and cut into wedges lengthwise
- 1 tablespoon olive oil
- 2 teaspoons seasoning salt (recipe below)

Directions:

1. Preheat the air fryer to 400°F.
2. Toss the potatoes with the olive oil and the seasoning salt.

3. Air-fry for 20 minutes (depending on the size of the wedges), turning the potatoes over gently a few times throughout the cooking process to brown and cook them evenly.

Okra

Servings: 4
Cooking Time: 12 Minutes

Ingredients:

- 7–8 ounces fresh okra
- 1 egg
- 1 cup milk
- 1 cup breadcrumbs
- ½ teaspoon salt
- oil for misting or cooking spray

Directions:

1. Remove stem ends from okra and cut in ½-inch slices.
2. In a medium bowl, beat together egg and milk. Add okra slices and stir to coat.
3. In a sealable plastic bag or container with lid, mix together the breadcrumbs and salt.
4. Remove okra from egg mixture, letting excess drip off, and transfer into bag with breadcrumbs.
5. Shake okra in crumbs to coat well.
6. Place all of the coated okra into the air fryer basket and mist with oil or cooking spray. Okra doesn't need to cook in a single layer, nor is it necessary to spray all sides at this point. A good spritz on top will do.
7. Cook at 390°F for 5minutes. Shake basket to redistribute and give it another spritz as you shake.
8. Cook 5 more minutes. Shake and spray again. Cook for 2 minutes longer or until golden brown and crispy.

Street Corn

Servings: 4
Cooking Time: 10 Minutes

Ingredients:

- 1 tablespoon butter
- 4 ears corn
- ⅓ cup plain Greek yogurt
- 2 tablespoons Parmesan cheese
- ½ teaspoon paprika
- ½ teaspoon garlic powder
- ¼ teaspoon salt
- ¼ teaspoon black pepper
- ¼ cup finely chopped cilantro

Directions:

1. Preheat the air fryer to 400°F.
2. In a medium microwave-safe bowl, melt the butter in the microwave. Lightly brush the outside of the ears of corn with the melted butter.
3. Place the corn into the air fryer basket and cook for 5 minutes, flip the corn, and cook another 5 minutes.
4. Meanwhile, in a medium bowl, mix the yogurt, cheese, paprika, garlic powder, salt, and pepper. Set aside.
5. Carefully remove the corn from the air fryer and let cool 3 minutes. Brush the outside edges with the yogurt mixture and top with fresh chopped cilantro. Serve immediately.

Home Fries

Servings: 4
Cooking Time: 20 Minutes

Ingredients:

- 3 pounds potatoes, cut into 1-inch cubes
- ½ teaspoon oil
- salt and pepper

Directions:

1. In a large bowl, mix the potatoes and oil thoroughly.
2. Cook at 390°F for 10minutes and shake the basket to redistribute potatoes.
3. Cook for an additional 10 minutes, until brown and crisp.
4. Season with salt and pepper to taste.

Honey-mustard Roasted Cabbage

Servings: 4
Cooking Time: 35 Minutes

Ingredients:

- 4 cups chopped green cabbage
- 1/3 cup honey mustard dressing
- 1 shallot, chopped
- 2 garlic cloves, minced
- 2 tbsp olive oil
- 1 tbsp lemon juice
- 1 tbsp cornstarch
- ½ tsp fennel seeds

Directions:

1. Preheat the air fryer to 370°F.Toss the cabbage, shallot, olive oil and garlic in a cake pan. Bake for 10 minutes or until the cabbage is wilted, then drain the excess liquid. While the cabbage is cooking, combine the salad dressing, lemon juice, cornstarch, and fennel seeds in a bowl. Take cake pan out of the fryer and pour out any excess liquid. Pour the dressing mix over the drained cabbage and mix well. Return the pan to the fryer and Bake for 7-11 minutes more, stirring twice during cooking until the cabbage is tender and the sauce has thickened. Serve warm.

Hawaiian Brown Rice

Servings: 4
Cooking Time: 12 Minutes
Ingredients:

- ¼ pound ground sausage
- 1 teaspoon butter
- ¼ cup minced onion
- ¼ cup minced bell pepper
- 2 cups cooked brown rice
- 1 8-ounce can crushed pineapple, drained

Directions:

1. Shape sausage into 3 or 4 thin patties. Cook at 390°F for 6 to 8minutes or until well done. Remove from air fryer, drain, and crumble. Set aside.
2. Place butter, onion, and bell pepper in baking pan. Cook at 390°F for 1 minute and stir. Cook 4 minutes longer or just until vegetables are tender.
3. Add sausage, rice, and pineapple to vegetables and stir together.
4. Cook at 390°F for 2 minutes, until heated through.

Chicken Eggrolls

Servings: 10
Cooking Time: 17 Minutes
Ingredients:

- 1 tablespoon vegetable oil
- ¼ cup chopped onion
- 1 clove garlic, minced
- 1 cup shredded carrot
- ½ cup thinly sliced celery
- 2 cups cooked chicken
- 2 cups shredded white cabbage
- ½ cup teriyaki sauce
- 20 egg roll wrappers
- 1 egg, whisked
- 1 tablespoon water

Directions:

1. Preheat the air fryer to 390°F.
2. In a large skillet, heat the oil over medium-high heat. Add in the onion and sauté for 1 minute. Add in the garlic and sauté for 30 seconds. Add in the carrot and celery and cook for 2 minutes. Add in the chicken, cabbage, and teriyaki sauce. Allow the mixture to cook for 1 minute, stirring to combine. Remove from the heat.
3. In a small bowl, whisk together the egg and water for brushing the edges.
4. Lay the eggroll wrappers out at an angle. Place ¼ cup filling in the center. Fold the bottom corner up first and then fold in the corners; roll up to complete eggroll.
5. Place the eggrolls in the air fryer basket, spray with cooking spray, and cook for 8 minutes, turn over, and cook another 2 to 4 minutes.

Herbed Zucchini Poppers

Servings: 4
Cooking Time: 30 Minutes
Ingredients:

- 1 tbsp grated Parmesan cheese
- 2 zucchini, sliced
- 1 cup breadcrumbs
- 2 eggs, beaten
- Salt and pepper to taste
- 1 tsp dry tarragon
- 1 tsp dry dill

Directions:

1. Preheat air fryer to 390°F. Place the breadcrumbs, Parmesan, tarragon, dill, salt, and pepper in a bowl and stir to combine. Dip the zucchini into the beaten eggs, then coat with Parmesan-crumb mixture. Lay the zucchini slices on the greased frying basket in an even layer. Air Fry for 14-16 minutes, shaking the basket several times during cooking. When ready, the zucchini will be crispy and golden brown. Serve hot and enjoy!

Charred Radicchio Salad

Servings: 4
Cooking Time: 5 Minutes
Ingredients:

- 2 Small 5- to 6-ounce radicchio head(s)
- 3 tablespoons Olive oil
- ½ teaspoon Table salt
- 2 tablespoons Balsamic vinegar
- Up to ¼ teaspoon Red pepper flakes

Directions:

1. Preheat the air fryer to 375°F .
2. Cut the radicchio head(s) into quarters through the stem end. Brush the oil over the heads, particularly getting it between the leaves along the cut sides. Sprinkle the radicchio quarters with the salt.
3. When the machine is at temperature, set the quarters cut sides up in the basket with as much air space between them as possible. They should not touch. Air-fry undisturbed for 5 minutes, watching carefully because they burn quickly, until blackened in bits and soft.

4. Use a nonstick-safe spatula to transfer the quarters to a cutting board. Cool for a minute or two, then cut out the thick stems inside the heads. Discard these tough bits and chop the remaining heads into bite-size bits. Scrape them into a bowl. Add the vinegar and red pepper flakes. Toss well and serve warm.

Hasselbacks

Servings: 4
Cooking Time: 41 Minutes
Ingredients:

- 2 large potatoes (approx. 1 pound each)
- oil for misting or cooking spray
- salt, pepper, and garlic powder
- 1½ ounces sharp Cheddar cheese, sliced very thin
- ¼ cup chopped green onions
- 2 strips turkey bacon, cooked and crumbled
- light sour cream for serving (optional)

Directions:

1. Preheat air fryer to 390°F.
2. Scrub potatoes. Cut thin vertical slices ¼-inch thick crosswise about three-quarters of the way down so that bottom of potato remains intact.
3. Fan potatoes slightly to separate slices. Mist with oil and sprinkle with salt, pepper, and garlic powder to taste. Potatoes will be very stiff, but try to get some of the oil and seasoning between the slices.
4. Place potatoes in air fryer basket and cook for 40 minutes or until centers test done when pierced with a fork.
5. Top potatoes with cheese slices and cook for 30 seconds to 1 minute to melt cheese.
6. Cut each potato in half crosswise, and sprinkle with green onions and crumbled bacon. If you like, add a dollop of sour cream before serving.

Truffle Vegetable Croquettes

Servings: 4
Cooking Time: 40 Minutes
Ingredients:

- 2 cooked potatoes, mashed
- 1 cooked carrot, mashed
- 1 tbsp onion, minced
- 2 eggs, beaten
- 2 tbsp melted butter
- 1 tbsp truffle oil
- ½ tbsp flour
- Salt and pepper to taste

Directions:

1. Preheat air fryer to 350°F. Sift the flour, salt, and pepper in a bowl and stir to combine. Add the potatoes, carrot, onion, butter, and truffle oil to a separate bowl and mix well. Shape the potato mixture into small bite-sized patties. Dip the potato patties into the beaten eggs, coating thoroughly, then roll in the flour mixture to cover all sides. Arrange the croquettes in the greased frying basket and Air Fry for 14-16 minutes. Halfway through cooking, shake the basket. The croquettes should be crispy and golden. Serve hot and enjoy!

Fried Pearl Onions With Balsamic Vinegar And Basil

Servings: 2
Cooking Time: 10 Minutes
Ingredients:

- 1 pound fresh pearl onions
- 1 tablespoon olive oil
- salt and freshly ground black pepper
- 1 teaspoon high quality aged balsamic vinegar
- 1 tablespoon chopped fresh basil leaves (or mint)

Directions:

1. Preheat the air fryer to 400°F.
2. Decide whether you want to peel the onions before or after they cook. Peeling them ahead of time is a little more laborious. Peeling after they cook is easier, but a little messier since the onions are hot and you may discard more of the onion than you'd like to. If you opt to peel them first, trim the tiny root of the onions off and pinch off any loose papery skins. (It's ok if there are some skins left on the onions.) Toss the pearl onions with the olive oil, salt and freshly ground black pepper.
3. Air-fry for 10 minutes, shaking the basket a couple of times during the cooking process. (If your pearl onions are very large, you may need to add a couple of minutes to this cooking time.)
4. Let the onions cool slightly and then slip off any remaining skins.
5. Toss the onions with the balsamic vinegar and basil and serve.

Brussels Sprouts

Serving: 3
Cooking Time: 5 Minutes
Ingredients:

- 1 10-ounce package frozen brussels sprouts, thawed and halved
- 2 teaspoons olive oil
- salt and pepper

Directions:

1. Toss the brussels sprouts and olive oil together.
2. Place them in the air fryer basket and season to taste with salt and pepper.
3. Cook at 360°F for approximately 5minutes, until the edges begin to brown.

Hush Puppies

Servings: 8
Cooking Time: 11 Minutes
Ingredients:

- ½ cup Whole or low-fat milk (not fat-free)
- 1½ tablespoons Butter
- ½ cup plus 1 tablespoon, plus more All-purpose flour
- ½ cup plus 1 tablespoon Yellow cornmeal
- 2 teaspoons Granulated white sugar
- 2 teaspoons Baking powder
- ¾ teaspoon Baking soda
- ¾ teaspoon Table salt
- ¼ teaspoon Onion powder
- 3 tablespoons (or 1 medium egg, well beaten) Pasteurized egg substitute, such as Egg Beaters
- Vegetable oil spray

Directions:

1. Heat the milk and butter in a small saucepan set over medium heat just until the butter melts and the milk is steamy. Do not simmer or boil.
2. Meanwhile, whisk the flour, cornmeal, sugar, baking powder, baking soda, salt, and onion powder in a large bowl until the mixture is a uniform color.
3. Stir the hot milk mixture into the flour mixture to form a dough. Set aside to cool for 5 minutes.
4. Mix the egg substitute or egg into the dough to make a thick, smooth batter. Cover and refrigerate for at least 1 hour or up to 4 hours.
5. Preheat the air fryer to 350°F .
6. Lightly flour your clean, dry hands. Roll 2 tablespoons of the batter into a ball between your floured palms. Set aside, flour your hands again if necessary, and continue making more balls with the remaining batter.
7. Coat the balls all over with the vegetable oil spray. Line the machine's basket (or basket attachment) with a piece of parchment paper. Set the balls on the parchment paper with as much air space between them as possible. Air-fry for 9 minutes, or until lightly browned and set.
8. Use kitchen tongs to gently transfer the hush puppies to a wire rack. Cool for at least 5 minutes before serving. Or cool to room temperature, about 45 minutes, and store in a sealed container at room temperature for up to 2 days. To crisp the hush puppies again, put them in a 350°F air fryer for 2 minutes. (There's no need for parchment paper in the machine during reheating.)

Fried Eggplant Balls

Servings: 4
Cooking Time: 40 Minutes
Ingredients:

- 1 medium eggplant (about 1 pound)
- olive oil
- salt and freshly ground black pepper
- 1 cup grated Parmesan cheese
- 2 cups fresh breadcrumbs
- 2 tablespoons chopped fresh parsley
- 2 tablespoons chopped fresh basil
- 1 clove garlic, minced
- 1 egg, lightly beaten
- ½ cup fine dried breadcrumbs

Directions:

1. Preheat the air fryer to 400°F.
2. Quarter the eggplant by cutting it in half both lengthwise and horizontally. Make a few slashes in the flesh of the eggplant but not through the skin. Brush the cut surface of the eggplant generously with olive oil and transfer to the air fryer basket, cut side up. Air-fry for 10 minutes. Turn the eggplant quarters cut side down and air-fry for another 15 minutes or until the eggplant is soft all the way through. You may need to rotate the pieces in the air fryer so that they cook evenly. Transfer the eggplant to a cutting board to cool.
3. Place the Parmesan cheese, the fresh breadcrumbs, fresh herbs, garlic and egg in a food processor. Scoop the flesh out of the eggplant, discarding the skin and any pieces that are tough. You should have about 1 to 1½ cups of eggplant. Add the eggplant to the food processor and process everything together until

smooth. Season with salt and pepper. Refrigerate the mixture for at least 30 minutes.

4. Place the dried breadcrumbs into a shallow dish or onto a plate. Scoop heaping tablespoons of the eggplant mixture into the dried breadcrumbs. Roll the dollops of eggplant in the breadcrumbs and then shape into small balls. You should have 16 to 18 eggplant balls at the end. Refrigerate until you are ready to air-fry.

5. Preheat the air fryer to 350°F.

6. Spray the eggplant balls and the air fryer basket with olive oil. Air-fry the eggplant balls for 15 minutes, rotating the balls during the cooking process to brown evenly.

Sweet Potato Puffs

Servings: 18

Cooking Time: 35 Minutes

Ingredients:

- 3 8- to 10-ounce sweet potatoes
- 1 cup Seasoned Italian-style dried bread crumbs
- 3 tablespoons All-purpose flour
- 3 tablespoons Instant mashed potato flakes
- 3/4 teaspoon Onion powder
- 3/4 teaspoon Table salt
- Olive oil spray

Directions:

1. Preheat the air fryer to 350°F .
2. Prick the sweet potatoes in four or five different places with the tines of a flatware fork (not in a line but all around the sweet potatoes).
3. When the machine is at temperature, set the sweet potatoes in the basket with as much air space between them as possible. Air-fry undisturbed for 20 minutes.
4. Use kitchen tongs to transfer the sweet potatoes to a wire rack. (They will still be firm; they are only partially cooked.) Cool for 10 to 15 minutes. Meanwhile, increase the machine's temperature to 400°F. Spread the bread crumbs on a dinner plate.
5. Peel the sweet potatoes. Shred them through the large holes of a box grater into a large bowl. Stir in the flour, potato flakes, onion powder, and salt until well combined.
6. Scoop up 2 tablespoons of the sweet potato mixture. Form it into a small puff, a cylinder about like a Tater Tot. Set this cylinder in the bread crumbs. Gently roll it around to coat on all sides, even the ends. Set aside on a cutting board and continue making more puffs: 11 more for a small batch, 17 more for a medium batch, or 23 more for a large batch.
7. Generously coat the puffs with olive oil spray on all sides. Set the puffs in the basket with as much air space between them as possible. They should not be touching, but even a fraction of an inch will work well. Air-fry undisturbed for 15 minutes, or until lightly browned and crunchy.
8. Gently turn the contents of the basket out onto a wire rack. Cool the puffs for a couple of minutes before serving.

Crispy Brussels Sprouts

Servings: 3

Cooking Time: 12 Minutes

Ingredients:

- 1¼ pounds Medium, 2-inch-in-length Brussels sprouts
- 1½ tablespoons Olive oil
- ¾ teaspoon Table salt

Directions:

1. Preheat the air fryer to 400°F.
2. Halve each Brussels sprout through the stem end, pulling off and discarding any discolored outer leaves. Put the sprout halves in a large bowl, add the oil and salt, and stir well to coat evenly, until the Brussels sprouts are glistening.
3. When the machine is at temperature, scrape the contents of the bowl into the basket, gently spreading the Brussels sprout halves into as close to one layer as possible. Air-fry for 12 minutes, gently tossing and rearranging the vegetables twice to get all covered or touching parts exposed to the air currents, until crisp and browned at the edges.
4. Gently pour the contents of the basket onto a wire rack. Cool for a minute or two before serving.

Patatas Bravas

Servings: 4

Cooking Time: 35 Minutes

Ingredients:

- 1 lb baby potatoes
- 1 onion, chopped
- 4 garlic cloves, minced
- 2 jalapeño peppers, minced
- 2 tsp olive oil
- 2 tsp Chile de Árbol, ground
- ½ tsp ground cumin
- ½ tsp dried oregano

Directions:

1. Preheat air fryer to 370°F. Put the baby potatoes, onion, garlic, and jalapeños in a bowl, stir, then pour in the olive oil and stir again to coat. Season with ground chile de Árbol, cumin, and oregano, and stir once again. Put the bowl in the air fryer and Air Fry for 22-28 minutes, shake the bowl once. Serve hot.

Simple Baked Potatoes With Dill Yogurt

Servings: 4
Cooking Time: 45 Minutes
Ingredients:

- 4 Yukon gold potatoes
- Salt and black pepper
- ½ cup Greek yogurt
- ¼ cup minced dill

Directions:

1. Pierce the potatoes with a fork. Lightly coat them with sprays of cooking oil, then season with salt. Preheat air fryer to 400°F. Air Fry the potatoes in the greased frying basket for 30-35 minutes, flipping once halfway through cooking until completely cooked and slightly crispy. A knife will cut into the center of the potato with ease. Remove them to a serving dish. Add toppings of yogurt, dill, salt, and pepper to taste.

Roasted Belgian Endive With Pistachios And Lemon

Servings: 2
Cooking Time: 7 Minutes
Ingredients:

- 2 Medium 3-ounce Belgian endive head(s)
- 2 tablespoons Olive oil
- ½ teaspoon Table salt
- ¼ cup Finely chopped unsalted shelled pistachios
- Up to 2 teaspoons Lemon juice

Directions:

1. Preheat the air fryer to 325°F (or 330°F, if that's the closest setting).
2. Trim the Belgian endive head(s), removing the little bit of dried-out stem end but keeping the leaves intact. Quarter the head(s) through the stem (which will hold the leaves intact). Brush the endive quarters with oil, getting it down between the leaves. Sprinkle the quarters with salt.
3. When the machine is at temperature, set the endive quarters cut sides up in the basket with as much air space between them as possible. They should not touch. Air-fry undisturbed for 7 minutes, or until lightly browned along the edges.
4. Use kitchen tongs to transfer the endive quarters to serving plates or a platter. Sprinkle with the pistachios and lemon juice. Serve warm or at room temperature.

Teriyaki Tofu With Spicy Mayo

Servings: 2
Cooking Time: 35 Minutes + 1 Hour To Marinate
Ingredients:

- 1 scallion, chopped
- 7 oz extra-firm tofu, sliced
- 2 tbsp soy sauce
- 1 tsp toasted sesame oil
- 1 red chili, thinly sliced
- 1 tsp mirin
- 1 tsp light brown sugar
- 1 garlic clove, grated
- ½ tsp grated ginger
- 1/3 cup sesame seeds
- 1 egg
- 4 tsp mayonnaise
- 1 tbsp lime juice
- 1 tsp hot chili powder

Directions:

1. Squeeze most of the water from the tofu by lightly pressing the slices between two towels. Place the tofu in a baking dish. Use a whisk to mix soy sauce, sesame oil, red chili, mirin, brown sugar, garlic and ginger. Pour half of the marinade over the tofu. Using a spatula, carefully flip the tofu down and pour the other half of the marinade over. Refrigerate for 1 hour.
2. Preheat air fryer to 400°F. In a shallow plate, add sesame seeds. In another shallow plate, beat the egg. Remove the tofu from the refrigerator. Let any excess marinade drip off. Dip each piece in the egg mixture and then in the sesame seeds. Transfer to greased frying basket. Air Fry for 10 minutes, flipping once until toasted and crispy. Meanwhile, mix mayonnaise, lime juice, and hot chili powder and in a small bowl. Top with a dollop of hot chili mayo and some scallions. Serve and enjoy!

Rich Spinach Chips

Servings: 4
Cooking Time: 20 Minutes
Ingredients:

- 10 oz spinach
- 2 tbsp lemon juice
- 2 tbsp olive oil
- Salt and pepper to taste
- ½ tsp garlic powder
- ½ tsp onion powder

Directions:

1. Preheat air fryer to 350°F. Place the spinach in a bowl, and drizzle with lemon juice and olive oil and massage with your hands. Scatter with salt, pepper, garlic, and onion and gently toss to coat well. Arrange the leaves in a single layer and Bake for 3 minutes. Shake and Bake for another 1-3 minutes until brown. Let cool completely.

Roasted Cauliflower With Garlic And Capers

Servings: 3

Cooking Time: 10 Minutes

Ingredients:

- 3 cups (about 15 ounces) 1-inch cauliflower florets
- 2 tablespoons Olive oil
- 1½ tablespoons Drained and rinsed capers, chopped
- 2 teaspoons Minced garlic
- ¼ teaspoon Table salt
- Up to ¼ teaspoon Red pepper flakes

Directions:

1. Preheat the air fryer to 375°F .
2. Stir the cauliflower florets, olive oil, capers, garlic, salt, and red pepper flakes in a large bowl until the florets are evenly coated.
3. When the machine is at temperature, put the florets in the basket, spreading them out to as close to one layer as you can. Air-fry for 10 minutes, tossing once to get any covered pieces exposed to the air currents, until tender and lightly browned.
4. Dump the contents of the basket into a serving bowl or onto a serving platter. Cool for a minute or two before serving.

Buttery Rolls

Servings: 6

Cooking Time: 14 Minutes

Ingredients:

- 6½ tablespoons Room-temperature whole or low-fat milk
- 3 tablespoons plus 1 teaspoon Butter, melted and cooled
- 3 tablespoons plus 1 teaspoon (or 1 medium egg, well beaten) Pasteurized egg substitute, such as Egg Beaters
- 1½ tablespoons Granulated white sugar
- 1¼ teaspoons Instant yeast
- ¼ teaspoon Table salt
- 2 cups, plus more for dusting All-purpose flour
- Vegetable oil
- Additional melted butter, for brushing

Directions:

1. Stir the milk, melted butter, pasteurized egg substitute (or whole egg), sugar, yeast, and salt in a medium bowl to combine. Stir in the flour just until the mixture makes a soft dough.
2. Lightly flour a clean, dry work surface. Turn the dough out onto the work surface. Knead the dough for 5 minutes to develop the gluten.
3. Lightly oil the inside of a clean medium bowl. Gather the dough into a compact ball and set it in the bowl. Turn the dough over so that its surface has oil on it all over. Cover the bowl tightly with plastic wrap and set aside in a warm, draft-free place until the dough has doubled in bulk, about 1½ hours.
4. Punch down the dough, then turn it out onto a clean, dry work surface. Divide it into 5 even balls for a small batch, 6 balls for a medium batch, or 8 balls for a large one.
5. For a small batch, lightly oil the inside of a 6-inch round cake pan and set the balls around its perimeter, separating them as much as possible.
6. For a medium batch, lightly oil the inside of a 7-inch round cake pan and set the balls in it with one ball at its center, separating them as much as possible.
7. For a large batch, lightly oil the inside of an 8-inch round cake pan and set the balls in it with one at the center, separating them as much as possible.
8. Cover with plastic wrap and set aside to rise for 30 minutes.
9. Preheat the air fryer to 350°F .
10. Uncover the pan and brush the rolls with a little melted butter, perhaps ½ teaspoon per roll. When the machine is at temperature, set the cake pan in the basket. Air-fry undisturbed for 14 minutes, or until the rolls have risen and browned.
11. Using kitchen tongs and a nonstick-safe spatula, two hot pads, or silicone baking mitts, transfer the cake pan from the basket to a wire rack. Cool the rolls in the pan for a minute or two. Turn the rolls out onto a wire rack, set them top side up again, and cool for at least another couple of minutes before serving warm.

Rich Baked Sweet Potatoes

Servings: 2
Cooking Time: 55 Minutes
Ingredients:

- 1 lb sweet potatoes, scrubbed and perforated with a fork
- 2 tsp olive oil
- Salt and pepper to taste
- 2 tbsp butter
- 3 tbsp honey

Directions:

1. Preheat air fryer at 400°F. Mix olive oil, salt, black pepper, and honey. Brush with the prepared mix over both sweet potatoes. Place them in the frying basket and Bake for 45 minutes, turning at 30 minutes mark. Let cool on a cutting board for 10 minutes until cool enough to handle. Slice each potato lengthwise. Press ends of one potato together to open up the slices. Top with butter to serve.

Greek-inspired Ratatouille

Servings: 6
Cooking Time: 55 Minutes
Ingredients:

- 1 cup cherry tomatoes
- ½ bulb fennel, finely sliced
- 2 russet potatoes, cubed
- ½ cup tomatoes, cubed
- 1 eggplant, cubed
- 1 zucchini, cubed
- 1 red onion, chopped
- 1 red bell pepper, chopped
- 2 garlic cloves, minced
- 1 tsp dried mint
- 1 tsp dried parsley
- 1 tsp dried oregano
- Salt and pepper to taste
- ¼ tsp red pepper flakes
- 1/3 cup olive oil
- 1 can tomato paste
- ¼ cup vegetable broth

Directions:

1. Preheat air fryer to 320°F. Mix the potatoes, tomatoes, fennel, eggplant, zucchini, onion, bell pepper, garlic, mint, parsley, oregano, salt, black pepper, and red pepper flakes in a bowl. Whisk the olive oil, tomato paste, broth, and ¼ cup of water in a small bowl. Toss the mixture with the vegetables.
2. Pour the coated vegetables into the air frying basket in a single layer and Roast for 20 minutes. Stir well and spread out again. Roast for an additional 10 minutes, then repeat the process and cook for another 10 minutes. Serve and enjoy!

Mushrooms

Servings: 4
Cooking Time: 12 Minutes
Ingredients:

- 8 ounces whole white button mushrooms
- ½ teaspoon salt
- ⅛ teaspoon pepper
- ¼ teaspoon garlic powder
- ¼ teaspoon onion powder
- 5 tablespoons potato starch
- 1 egg, beaten
- ¾ cup panko breadcrumbs
- oil for misting or cooking spray

Directions:

1. Place mushrooms in a large bowl. Add the salt, pepper, garlic and onion powders, and stir well to distribute seasonings.
2. Add potato starch to mushrooms and toss in bowl until well coated.
3. Dip mushrooms in beaten egg, roll in panko crumbs, and mist with oil or cooking spray.
4. Place mushrooms in air fryer basket. You can cook them all at once, and it's okay if a few are stacked.
5. Cook at 390°F for 5minutes. Shake basket, then continue cooking for 7 more minutes, until golden brown and crispy.

Sticky Broccoli Florets

Servings: 4
Cooking Time: 20 Minutes
Ingredients:

- 4 cups broccoli florets
- 2 tbsp olive oil
- ½ tsp salt
- ½ cup grapefruit juice
- 1 tbsp raw honey
- 4-6 grapefruit wedges

Directions:

1. Preheat air fryer to 360°F. Add the broccoli, olive oil, salt, grapefruit juice, and honey to a bowl. Toss the broccoli in the liquid until well coated. Pour the broccoli mixture into the frying basket and Roast for 12 minutes, stirring once. Serve with grapefruit wedges.

Vegetable Roast

Servings: 6
Cooking Time: 20 Minutes

Ingredients:

- 2 tbsp dill, chopped
- 2 zucchini, cubed
- 1 red bell pepper, diced
- 2 garlic cloves, sliced
- 2 tbsp olive oil
- ½ tsp salt
- ½ tsp red pepper flakes

Directions:

1. Preheat air fryer to 380°F. Combine the zucchini, bell pepper, red pepper flakes, dill and garlic with olive oil and salt in a bowl. Pour the mixture into the frying basket and Roast for 14-16 minutes, shaking once. Serve warm.

Yukon Gold Potato Purée

Servings: 4
Cooking Time: 25 Minutes

Ingredients:

- 1 lb Yukon Gold potatoes, scrubbed and cubed
- 2 tbsp butter, melted
- Salt and pepper to taste
- 1/8 cup whole milk
- ¼ cup cream cheese
- 1 tbsp butter, softened
- ¼ cup chopped dill

Directions:

1. Preheat air fryer at 350°F. Toss the potatoes and melted butter in a bowl, place them in the frying basket, and Air Fry for 13-15 minutes, tossing once. Transfer them into a bowl. Using a fork, mash the potatoes. Stir in salt, pepper, half of the milk, cream cheese, and 1 tbsp of butter until you reach your desired consistency. Garnish with dill to serve.

Pecorino Dill Muffins

Servings:4
Cooking Time: 25 Minutes

Ingredients:

- ¼ cup grated Pecorino cheese
- 1 cup flour
- 1 tsp dried dill
- ⅛ tsp salt
- ¼ tsp onion powder
- 2 tsp baking powder
- 1 egg
- ¼ cup Greek yogurt

Directions:

1. Preheat air fryer to 350°F. In a bowl, combine dry the ingredients. Set aside. In another bowl, whisk the wet ingredients. Add the wet ingredients to the dry ingredients and combine until blended.
2. Transfer the batter to 6 silicone muffin cups lightly greased with olive oil. Place muffin cups in the frying basket and Bake for 12 minutes. Serve right away.

Roasted Bell Peppers With Garlic & Dill

Servings: 4
Cooking Time: 30 Minutes

Ingredients:

- 4 bell peppers, seeded and cut into fourths
- 1 tsp olive oil
- 4 garlic cloves, minced
- ½ tsp dried dill

Directions:

1. Preheat air fryer to 350°F. Add the peppers to the frying basket, spritz with olive oil, shake, and Roast for 15 minutes. Season with garlic and dill, then cook for an additional 3-5 minutes. The veggies should be soft. Serve.

Crunchy Roasted Potatoes

Servings: 5
Cooking Time: 25 Minutes

Ingredients:

- 2 pounds Small (1- to 1½-inch-diameter) red, white, or purple potatoes
- 2 tablespoons Olive oil
- 2 teaspoons Table salt
- ¾ teaspoon Garlic powder
- ½ teaspoon Ground black pepper

Directions:

1. Preheat the air fryer to 400°F.
2. Toss the potatoes, oil, salt, garlic powder, and pepper in a large bowl until the spuds are evenly and thoroughly coated.
3. When the machine is at temperature, pour the potatoes into the basket, spreading them into an even layer (although they may be stacked on top of each other). Air-fry for 25 minutes, tossing twice, until the potatoes are tender but crunchy.
4. Pour the contents of the basket into a serving bowl. Cool for 5 minutes before serving.

Toasted Choco-nuts

Servings: 2
Cooking Time: 10 Minutes

Ingredients:

- 2 cups almonds
- 2 tsp maple syrup
- 2 tbsp cacao powder

Directions:

1. Preheat air fryer to 350°F. Distribute the almonds in a single layer in the frying basket and Bake for 3 minutes. Shake the basket and Bake for another 1 minute until golden brown. Remove them to a bowl. Drizzle with maple syrup and toss. Sprinkle with cacao powder and toss until well coated. Let cool completely. Store in a container at room temperature for up to 2 weeks or in the fridge for up to a month.

Chicken Salad With Sunny Citrus Dressing

Servings: 4
Cooking Time: 8 Minutes

Ingredients:

- Sunny Citrus Dressing
- 1 cup first cold-pressed extra virgin olive oil
- ⅓ cup red wine vinegar
- 2 tablespoons all natural orange marmalade
- 1 teaspoon dry mustard
- 1 teaspoon ground black pepper
- California Chicken
- 4 large chicken tenders
- 1 teaspoon olive oil
- juice of 1 small orange or clementine
- salt and pepper
- ½ teaspoon rosemary
- Salad
- 8 cups romaine or leaf lettuce, chopped or torn into bite-size pieces
- 2 clementines or small oranges, peeled and sectioned
- ½ cup dried cranberries
- 4 tablespoons sliced almonds

Directions:

1. In a 2-cup jar or container with lid, combine all dressing ingredients and shake until well blended. Refrigerate for at least 30minutes for flavors to blend.
2. Brush chicken tenders lightly with oil.
3. Drizzle orange juice over chicken.
4. Sprinkle with salt and pepper to taste.
5. Crush the rosemary and sprinkle over chicken.
6. Cook at 390°F for 3minutes, turn over, and cook for an additional 5 minutes or until chicken is tender and juices run clear.
7. When ready to serve, toss lettuce with 2 tablespoons of dressing to coat.
8. Divide lettuce among 4 plates or bowls. Arrange chicken and clementines on top and sprinkle cranberries and almonds. Pass extra dressing at the table.

Appetizers And Snacks Recipes

Za'atar Garbanzo Beans

Servings: 6
Cooking Time: 12 Minutes

Ingredients:

- One 14.5-ounce can garbanzo beans, drained and rinsed
- 1 tablespoon extra-virgin olive oil
- 6 teaspoons za'atar seasoning mix
- 2 tablespoons chopped parsley
- Salt and pepper, to taste

Directions:

1. Preheat the air fryer to 390°F.
2. In a medium bowl, toss the garbanzo beans with olive oil and za'atar seasoning.
3. Pour the beans into the air fryer basket and cook for 12 minutes, or until toasted as you like. Stir every 3 minutes while roasting.
4. Remove the beans from the air fryer basket into a serving bowl, top with fresh chopped parsley, and season with salt and pepper.

Honey-mustard Chicken Wings

Servings: 2
Cooking Time: 14 Minutes
Ingredients:

- 2 pounds chicken wings
- salt and freshly ground black pepper
- 2 tablespoons butter
- ¼ cup honey
- ¼ cup spicy brown mustard
- pinch ground cayenne pepper
- 2 teaspoons Worcestershire sauce

Directions:

1. Prepare the chicken wings by cutting off the wing tips and discarding (or freezing for chicken stock). Divide the drumettes from the wingettes by cutting through the joint. Place the chicken wing pieces in a large bowl.
2. Preheat the air fryer to 400°F.
3. Season the wings with salt and freshly ground black pepper and air-fry the wings in two batches for 10 minutes per batch, shaking the basket half way through the cooking process.
4. While the wings are air-frying, combine the remaining ingredients in a small saucepan over low heat.
5. When both batches are done, toss all the wings with the honey-mustard sauce and toss them all back into the basket for another 4 minutes to heat through and finish cooking. Give the basket a good shake part way through the cooking process to redistribute the wings. Remove the wings from the air fryer and serve.

Root Vegetable Crisps

Servings: 4
Cooking Time: 8 Minutes
Ingredients:

- 1 small taro root, peeled and washed
- 1 small yucca root, peeled and washed
- 1 small purple sweet potato, washed
- 2 cups filtered water
- 2 teaspoons extra-virgin olive oil
- ½ teaspoon salt

Directions:

1. Using a mandolin, slice the taro root, yucca root, and purple sweet potato into ⅛-inch slices.
2. Add the water to a large bowl. Add the sliced vegetables and soak for at least 30 minutes.
3. Preheat the air fryer to 370°F.
4. Drain the water and pat the vegetables dry with a paper towel or kitchen cloth. Toss the vegetables with the olive oil and sprinkle with salt. Liberally spray the air fryer basket with olive oil mist.
5. Place the vegetables into the air fryer basket, making sure not to overlap the pieces.
6. Cook for 8 minutes, shaking the basket every 2 minutes, until the outer edges start to turn up and the vegetables start to brown. Remove from the basket and serve warm. Repeat with the remaining vegetable slices until all are cooked.

Crunchy Tortellini Bites

Servings: 5
Cooking Time: 10 Minutes
Ingredients:

- 10 ounces (about 2½ cups) Cheese tortellini
- ⅓ cup Yellow cornmeal
- ⅓ cup Seasoned Italian-style dried bread crumbs
- ⅓ cup (about 1 ounce) Finely grated Parmesan cheese
- 1 Large egg
- Olive oil spray

Directions:

1. Bring a large pot of water to a boil over high heat. Add the tortellini and cook for 3 minutes. Drain in a colander set in the sink, then spread out the tortellini on a large baking sheet and cool for 15 minutes.
2. Preheat the air fryer to 400°F.
3. Mix the cornmeal, bread crumbs, and cheese in a large zip-closed plastic bag.
4. Whisk the egg in a medium bowl until uniform. Add the tortellini and toss well to coat, even along the inside curve of the pasta. Use a slotted spoon or kitchen tongs to transfer 5 or 6 tortellini to the plastic bag, seal, and shake gently to coat thoroughly and evenly. Set the coated tortellini aside on a cutting board and continue coating the rest in the same way.
5. Generously coat the tortellini on all sides with the olive oil spray, then set them in one layer in the basket. Air-fry undisturbed for 10 minutes, gently tossing the basket and rearranging the tortellini at the 4- and 7-minute marks, until brown and crisp.
6. Pour the contents of the basket onto a wire rack. Cool for 5 minutes before serving.

Savory Eggplant Fries

Servings: 4
Cooking Time: 20 Minutes

Ingredients:

- 1 eggplant, sliced
- 2 ½ tbsp shoyu
- 2 tsp garlic powder
- 2 tsp onion powder
- 4 tsp olive oil
- 2 tbsp fresh basil, chopped

Directions:

1. Preheat air fryer to 390°F. Place the eggplant slices in a bowl and sprinkle the shoyu, garlic, onion, and oil on top. Coat the eggplant evenly. Place the eggplant in a single layer in the greased frying basket and Air Fry for 5 minutes. Remove and put the eggplant in the bowl again. Toss the eggplant slices to coat evenly with the remaining liquid and put back in the fryer. Roast for another 3 minutes. Remove the basket and flip the pieces over to ensure even cooking. Roast for another 5 minutes or until the eggplant is golden. Top with basil and serve.

Poutine

Servings: 2
Cooking Time: 25 Minutes

Ingredients:

- 2 russet potatoes, scrubbed and cut into ½-inch sticks
- 2 teaspoons vegetable oil
- 2 tablespoons butter
- ¼ onion, minced (about ¼ cup)
- 1 clove garlic, smashed
- ¼ teaspoon dried thyme
- 3 tablespoons flour
- 1 teaspoon tomato paste
- 1½ cups strong beef stock
- salt and lots of freshly ground black pepper
- a few dashes of Worcestershire sauce
- ⅔ cup chopped string cheese or cheese curds

Directions:

1. Bring a large saucepan of salted water to a boil on the stovetop while you peel and cut the potatoes. Blanch the potatoes in the boiling salted water for 4 minutes while you Preheat the air fryer to 400°F. Strain the potatoes and rinse them with cold water. Dry them well with a clean kitchen towel.
2. Toss the dried potato sticks gently with the oil and place them in the air fryer basket. Air-fry for 25 minutes, shaking the basket a few times while the fries cook to help them brown evenly.
3. While the fries are cooking, make the gravy. Melt the butter in a small saucepan over medium heat. Add the onion, garlic and thyme and cook for five minutes, until soft and just starting to brown. Stir in the flour and cook for another two minutes, stirring regularly. Finally, add the tomato paste and continue to cook for another minute or two. Whisk in the beef stock and bring the mixture to a boil to thicken. Season to taste with salt, lots of freshly ground black pepper and a few dashes of Worcestershire sauce. Keep the gravy warm.
4. As soon as the fries are done, season them with salt and transfer to a plate or basket. Top the fries with the cheese curds or string cheese, and pour the warm gravy over the top.

Enchilada Chicken Dip

Servings:6
Cooking Time: 20 Minutes

Ingredients:

- 1 cup chopped cooked chicken breasts
- 1 can diced green chiles, including juice
- 8 oz cream cheese, softened
- ¼ cup mayonnaise
- ¼ cup sour cream
- 2 tbsp chopped onion
- 1 jalapeño pepper, minced
- 1 cup shredded mozzarella
- ¼ cup diced tomatoes
- 1 tsp chili powder

Directions:

1. Preheat air fryer to 400°F. Beat the cream cheese, mayonnaise, and sour cream in a bowl until smooth. Stir in the cooked chicken, onion, green chiles, jalapeño, and ½ cup of mozzarella cheese. Spoon the mixture into a baking dish. Sprinkle the remaining cheese on top, and place the dish in the fryer. Bake for 10 minutes. Garnish the dip with diced tomatoes and chili powder. Serve.

Crunchy Pickle Chips

Servings: 4
Cooking Time: 20 Minutes
Ingredients:

- 1 lb dill pickles, sliced
- 2 eggs
- 1/3 cup flour
- 1/3 cup bread crumbs
- 1 tsp Italian seasoning

Directions:

1. Preheat air fryer to 400°F. Set out three small bowls. In the first bowl, add flour. In the second bowl, beat eggs. In the third bowl, mix bread crumbs with Italian seasoning. Dip the pickle slices in the flour. Shake, then dredge in egg. Roll in bread crumbs and shake excess. Place the pickles in the greased frying basket and Air Fry for 6 minutes. Flip them halfway through cooking and fry for another 3 minutes until crispy. Serve warm.

Roasted Jalapeño Salsa Verde

Servings:4
Cooking Time: 20 Minutes
Ingredients:

- ¾ lb fresh tomatillos, husked
- 1 jalapeño, stem removed
- 4 green onions, sliced
- 3 garlic cloves, peeled
- ½ tsp salt
- 1 tsp lime juice
- ¼ tsp apple cider vinegar
- ¼ cup cilantro leaves

Directions:

1. Preheat air fryer to 400°F. Add tomatillos and jalapeño to the frying basket and Bake for 5 minutes. Put in green onions and garlic and Bake for 5 more minutes. Transfer it into a food processor along with salt, lime juice, vinegar and cilantro and blend until the sauce is finely chopped. Pour it into a small sealable container and refrigerate it until ready to use up to five days.

Crab Rangoon

Servings: 18
Cooking Time: 6 Minutes
Ingredients:

- 4½ tablespoons (a little more than ¼ pound) Crabmeat, preferably backfin or claw, picked over for shells and cartilage
- 1½ ounces (3 tablespoons) Regular or low-fat cream cheese (not fat-free), softened to room temperature
- 1½ tablespoons Minced scallion
- 1½ teaspoons Minced garlic
- 1½ teaspoons Worcestershire sauce
- 18 Wonton wrappers (thawed, if necessary)
- Vegetable oil spray

Directions:

1. Preheat the air fryer to 400°F.
2. Gently stir the crab, cream cheese, scallion, garlic, and Worcestershire sauce in a medium bowl until well combined.
3. Set a bowl of water on a clean, dry work surface or next to a large cutting board. Set one wonton wrapper on the surface, then put a teaspoonful of the crab mixture in the center of the wrapper. Dip your clean finger in the water and run it around the edge of the wrapper. Bring all four sides up to the center and over the filling, and pinch them together in the middle to seal without covering all of the filling. The traditional look is for the corners of the filled wonton to become four open “flower petals” radiating out from the filled center. Set the filled wonton aside and continue making more as needed. (If you want a video tutorial on filling these, see ours at our YouTube channel, Cooking with Bruce and Mark.)
4. Generously coat the filled wontons with vegetable oil spray. Set them sealed side up in the basket with a little room among them. Air-fry undisturbed for 6 minutes, or until golden brown and crisp.
5. Use a nonstick-safe spatula to gently transfer the wontons to a wire rack. Cool for 5 minutes before serving warm.

Fiery Cheese Sticks

Servings: 4
Cooking Time: 20 Minutes + Freezing Time
Ingredients:

- 1 egg, beaten
- ½ cup dried bread crumbs
- ¼ cup ground peanuts
- 1 tbsp chili powder
- ¼ tsp ground coriander
- ¼ tsp red pepper flakes
- ⅛ tsp cayenne pepper
- 8 mozzarella cheese sticks

Directions:

1. Preheat the air fryer to 375°F. Beat the egg in a bowl, and on a plate, combine the breadcrumbs,

peanuts, coriander, chili powder, pepper flakes, and cayenne. Dip each piece of string cheese in the egg, then in the breadcrumb mix. After lining a baking sheet with parchment paper, put the sticks on it and freeze them for 30 minutes. Get the sticks out of the freezer and set in the frying basket in a single layer. Spritz them with cooking oil. Air Fry for 7-9 minutes until the exterior is golden and the interior is hot and melted. Serve hot with marinara or ranch sauce.

Fried Gyoza

Servings: 18

Cooking Time: 6 Minutes

Ingredients:

- 5 ounces Lean ground pork
- 2½ tablespoons Very thinly sliced scallion
- 1 tablespoon plus 2 teaspoons Minced peeled fresh ginger
- 1¼ teaspoons Toasted sesame oil
- ⅛ teaspoon Table salt
- ⅛ teaspoon Ground black pepper
- 18 Round gyoza or square wonton wrappers (thawed, if necessary)
- Vegetable oil spray

Directions:

1. Preheat the air fryer to 350°F .
2. Mix the ground pork, scallion, ginger, sesame oil, salt, and pepper in a bowl until well combined.
3. Set a bowl of water on a clean, dry surface or next to a clean, dry cutting board. Set one gyoza or wonton wrapper on that surface. Dip your clean finger in the water and run it around the perimeter of the gyoza wrapper or the edge of the wonton wrapper. Put about 1 ½ teaspoons of the meat mixture in the center of the wrapper.
4. For the gyoza wrapper, fold the wrapper in half to close, pressing the edge to seal, then wet the outside of the edge of both sides of the seam and pleat it into little ridges to seal.
5. For the wonton wrapper, fold it in half lengthwise to make a rectangle, then seal the sides together, flattening the packet a bit as you do.
6. Set the filled wrapper aside and continue making more in the same way. When done, generously coat them on all sides with vegetable oil spray.
7. Place the gyoza in the basket in one layer and air-fry undisturbed for 6 minutes, or until browned and crisp at the edges.
8. Use kitchen tongs or a nonstick-safe spatula to gently transfer the gyoza to a wire rack. Cool for only 2 or 3 minutes before serving hot.

Prosciutto Polenta Rounds

Servings: 6

Cooking Time: 40 Minutes + 10 Minutes To Cool

Ingredients:

- 1 tube precooked polenta
- 1 tbsp garlic oil
- 4 oz cream cheese, softened
- 3 tbsp mayonnaise
- 2 scallions, sliced
- 1 tbsp minced fresh chives
- 6 prosciutto slices, chopped

Directions:

1. Preheat the air fryer to 400°F. Slice the polenta crosswise into 12 rounds. Brush both sides of each round with garlic oil and put 6 of them in the frying basket. Put a rack in the basket over the polenta and add the other 6 rounds. Bake for 15 minutes, flip, and cook for 10-15 more minutes or until the polenta is crispy and golden. While the polenta is cooking, beat the cream cheese and mayo and stir in the scallions, chives, and prosciutto. When the polenta is cooked, lay out on a wire rack to cool for 15 minutes. Top with the cream cheese mix and serve.

Basil Feta Crostini

Servings: 4

Cooking Time: 10 Minutes

Ingredients:

- 1 baguette, sliced
- ¼ cup olive oil
- 2 garlic cloves, minced
- 4 oz feta cheese
- 2 tbsp basil, minced

Directions:

1. Preheat air fryer to 380°F. Combine together the olive oil and garlic in a bowl. Brush it over one side of each slice of bread. Put the bread in a single layer in the frying basket and Bake for 5 minutes. In a small bowl, mix together the feta cheese and basil. Remove the toast from the air fryer, then spread a thin layer of the goat cheese mixture over the top of each piece. Serve.

Herbed Cauliflower

Servings: 4
Cooking Time: 15 Minutes
Ingredients:

- 2 cups cauliflower florets
- 2 tsp olive oil
- 4 garlic cloves, minced
- Salt and pepper to taste
- ½ tsp onion powder
- 1 tsp smoked paprika
- ½ tsp dried rosemary
- ½ tsp dried thyme
- ½ tsp dried oregano
- ¼ tsp ground sage
- 1 tbsp chopped parsley

Directions:

1. Preheat air fryer to 375°F. Toss cauliflower and all of the ingredients in a large bowl until coated. Arrange the cauliflower on the frying basket in a single layer. Roast for 5 minutes, then shake the basket. Roast for another 5 minutes until fork tender. Serve sprinkled with parsley.

Garlic Breadsticks

Servings: 12
Cooking Time: 7 Minutes
Ingredients:

- 1½ tablespoons Olive oil
- 1½ teaspoons Minced garlic
- ¼ teaspoon Table salt
- ¼ teaspoon Ground black pepper
- 6 ounces Purchased pizza dough (vegan dough, if that's a concern)

Directions:

1. Preheat the air fryer to 400°F. Mix the oil, garlic, salt, and pepper in a small bowl.
2. Divide the pizza dough into 4 balls for a small air fryer, 6 for a medium machine, or 8 for a large, each ball about the size of a walnut in its shell. (Each should weigh 1 ounce, if you want to drag out a scale and get obsessive.) Roll each ball into a 5-inch-long stick under your clean palms on a clean, dry work surface. Brush the sticks with the oil mixture.
3. When the machine is at temperature, place the prepared dough sticks in the basket, leaving a 1-inch space between them. Air-fry undisturbed for 7 minutes, or until puffed, golden, and set to the touch.
4. Use kitchen tongs to gently transfer the breadsticks to a wire rack and repeat step 3 with the remaining dough sticks.

Hot Cauliflower Bites

Servings: 4
Cooking Time: 35 Minutes
Ingredients:

- 1 head cauliflower, cut into florets
- 1 cup all-purpose flour
- 1 tsp garlic powder
- 1/3 cup cayenne sauce

Directions:

1. Preheat air fryer to 370°F. Mix the flour, 1 cup of water, and garlic powder in a large bowl until a batter forms. Coat cauliflower in the batter, then transfer to a large bowl to drain excess. Place the cauliflower in the greased frying basket without stacking. Spray with cooking, then Bake for 6 minutes. Remove from the air fryer and transfer to a large bowl. Top with cayenne sauce. Return to the fryer and cook for 6 minutes or until crispy. Serve.

Salty Pita Crackers

Servings: 2
Cooking Time: 15 Minutes
Ingredients:

- 2 pitas, cut into wedges
- 1 tbsp olive oil
- ½ tsp garlic salt
- ¼ tsp paprika

Directions:

1. Preheat air fryer to 360°F. Coat the pita wedges with olive oil, paprika and garlic salt in a bowl. Put them into the frying basket and Air Fry for 6-8 minutes. Serve warm.

Green Olive And Mushroom Tapenade

Servings: 1
Cooking Time: 10 Minutes
Ingredients:

- ¾ pound Brown or Baby Bella mushrooms, sliced
- 1½ cups (about ½ pound) Pitted green olives
- 3 tablespoons Olive oil
- 1½ tablespoons Fresh oregano leaves, loosely packed
- ¼ teaspoon Ground black pepper

Directions:

1. Preheat the air fryer to 400°F.
2. When the machine is at temperature, arrange the mushroom slices in as close to an even layer as possible in the basket. They will overlap and even stack on top of each other.
3. Air-fry for 10 minutes, tossing the basket and rearranging the mushrooms every 2 minutes, until shriveled but with still-noticeable moisture.
4. Pour the mushrooms into a food processor. Add the olives, olive oil, oregano leaves, and pepper. Cover and process until grainy, not too much, just not fully smooth for better texture, stopping the machine at least once to scrape down the inside of the canister. Scrape the tapenade into a bowl and serve warm, or cover and refrigerate for up to 4 days. (The tapenade will taste better if it comes back to room temperature before serving.)

Cinnamon Apple Crisps

Servings: 1
Cooking Time: 22 Minutes

Ingredients:

- 1 large apple
- ½ teaspoon ground cinnamon
- 2 teaspoons avocado oil or coconut oil

Directions:

1. Preheat the air fryer to 300°F.
2. Using a mandolin or knife, slice the apples to ¼-inch thickness. Pat the apples dry with a paper towel or kitchen cloth. Sprinkle the apple slices with ground cinnamon. Spray or drizzle the oil over the top of the apple slices and toss to coat.
3. Place the apple slices in the air fryer basket. To allow for even cooking, don't overlap the slices; cook in batches if necessary.
4. Cook for 20 minutes, shaking the basket every 5 minutes. After 20 minutes, increase the air fryer temperature to 330°F and cook another 2 minutes, shaking the basket every 30 seconds. Remove the apples from the basket before they get too dark.
5. Spread the chips out onto paper towels to cool completely, at least 5 minutes. Repeat with the remaining apple slices until they're all cooked.

Tempura Fried Veggies

Servings: 4
Cooking Time: 6 Minutes

Ingredients:

- ½ cup all-purpose flour
- ½ teaspoon black pepper
- ¼ teaspoon salt
- 2 large eggs
- 1¼ cups panko breadcrumbs
- 1 tablespoon extra-virgin olive oil
- 1 cup white button mushrooms, cleaned
- 1 medium zucchini, skinned and sliced
- 1 medium carrot, skinned sliced

Directions:

1. Preheat the air fryer to 400°F.
2. In a small bowl, mix the flour, pepper, and salt.
3. In a separate bowl, whisk the eggs.
4. In a third bowl, mix together the breadcrumbs and olive oil.
5. Begin to batter the vegetables by placing them one at a time into the flour, then dipping them in the eggs, and coating them in breadcrumbs. When you've prepared enough to begin air frying, liberally spray the air fryer basket with olive oil and place the vegetables inside.
6. Cook for 6 minutes, or until the breadcrumb coating on the outside appears golden brown. Repeat coating the other vegetables while the first batch is cooking.
7. When the cooking completes, carefully remove the vegetables and keep them warm. Repeat cooking for the remaining vegetables until all are cooked.
8. Serve warm.

Yellow Onion Rings

Servings: 3
Cooking Time: 30 Minutes

Ingredients:

- ½ sweet yellow onion
- ½ cup buttermilk
- ¾ cup flour
- 1 tbsp cornstarch
- Salt and pepper to taste
- ¾ tsp garlic powder
- ½ tsp dried oregano
- 1 cup bread crumbs

Directions:

1. Preheat air fryer to 390°F. Cut the onion into ½-inch slices. Separate the onion slices into rings. Place the buttermilk in a bowl and set aside. In another bowl, combine the flour, cornstarch, salt, pepper, and garlic. Stir well and set aside. In a separate bowl, combine the breadcrumbs with oregano and salt.
2. Dip the rings into the buttermilk, dredge in flour, dip into the buttermilk again, and then coat into the crumb mixture. Put in the greased frying basket without overlapping. Spritz them with cooking oil and Air Fry for 13-16 minutes, shaking once or twice until the rings are crunchy and browned. Serve hot.

Bacon Candy

Servings: 6

Cooking Time: 6 Minutes

Ingredients:

- 1½ tablespoons Honey
- 1 teaspoon White wine vinegar
- 3 Extra thick–cut bacon strips, halved widthwise (gluten-free, if a concern)
- ½ teaspoon Ground black pepper

Directions:

1. Preheat the air fryer to 350°F .
2. Whisk the honey and vinegar in a small bowl until incorporated.
3. When the machine is at temperature, remove the basket. Lay the bacon strip halves in the basket in one layer. Brush the tops with the honey mixture; sprinkle each bacon strip evenly with black pepper.
4. Return the basket to the machine and air-fry undisturbed for 6 minutes, or until the bacon is crunchy. Or a little less time if you prefer bacon that's still pliable, an extra minute if you want the bacon super crunchy. Take care that the honey coating doesn't burn. Remove the basket from the machine and set aside for 5 minutes. Use kitchen tongs to transfer the bacon strips to a serving plate.

Spicy Sweet Potato Tater-tots

Servings: 6

Cooking Time: 10 Minutes

Ingredients:

- 6 cups filtered water
- 2 medium sweet potatoes, peeled and cut in half
- 1 teaspoon garlic powder
- ½ teaspoon black pepper, divided
- ½ teaspoon salt, divided
- 1 cup panko breadcrumbs
- 1 teaspoon blackened seasoning

Directions:

1. In a large stovetop pot, bring the water to a boil. Add the sweet potatoes and let boil about 10 minutes, until a metal fork prong can be inserted but the potatoes still have a slight give (not completely mashed).
2. Carefully remove the potatoes from the pot and let cool.
3. When you're able to touch them, grate the potatoes into a large bowl. Mix the garlic powder, ¼ teaspoon of the black pepper, and ¼ teaspoon of the salt into the potatoes. Place the mixture in the refrigerator and let set at least 45 minutes (if you're leaving them longer than 45 minutes, cover the bowl).
4. Before assembling, mix the breadcrumbs and blackened seasoning in a small bowl.
5. Remove the sweet potatoes from the refrigerator and preheat the air fryer to 400°F.
6. Assemble the tater-tots by using a teaspoon to portion batter evenly and form into a tater-tot shape. Roll each tater-tot in the breadcrumb mixture. Then carefully place the tater-tots in the air fryer basket. Be sure that you've liberally sprayed the air fryer basket with an olive oil mist. Repeat until tater-tots fill the basket without touching one another. You'll need to do multiple batches, depending on the size of your air fryer.
7. Cook the tater-tots for 3 to 6 minutes, flip, and cook another 3 to 6 minutes.
8. Remove from the air fryer carefully and keep warm until ready to serve.

Onion Puffs

Servings: 14

Cooking Time: 8 Minutes

Ingredients:

- Vegetable oil spray
- ¾ cup Chopped yellow or white onion
- ½ cup Seasoned Italian-style panko bread crumbs
- 4½ tablespoons All-purpose flour
- 4½ tablespoons Whole, low-fat, or fat-free milk
- 1½ tablespoons Yellow cornmeal
- 1¼ teaspoons Granulated white sugar
- ½ teaspoon Baking powder
- ¼ teaspoon Table salt

Directions:

1. Cut or tear a piece of aluminum foil so that it lines the air fryer's basket with a ½-inch space on each of its four sides. Lightly coat the foil with vegetable oil spray, then set the foil sprayed side up inside the basket.
2. Preheat the air fryer to 400°F.
3. Stir the onion, bread crumbs, flour, milk, cornmeal, sugar, baking powder, and salt in a bowl to form a thick batter.
4. Remove the basket from the machine. Drop the onion batter by 2-tablespoon measures onto the foil, spacing the mounds evenly across its surface. Return the basket to the machine and air-fry undisturbed for 4 minutes.
5. Remove the basket from the machine. Lightly coat the puffs with vegetable oil spray. Use kitchen tongs to pick up a corner of the foil, then gently pull it out of the

basket, letting the puffs slip onto the basket directly. Return the basket to the machine and continue air-frying undisturbed for 8 minutes, or until brown and crunchy.

6. Use kitchen tongs to transfer the puffs to a wire rack or a serving platter. Cool for 5 minutes before serving.

Cajun-spiced Pickle Chips

Servings: 4

Cooking Time: 20 Minutes

Ingredients:

- 16 oz canned pickle slices
- ½ cup flour
- 2 tbsp cornmeal
- 3 tsp Cajun seasoning
- 1 tbsp dried parsley
- 1 egg, beaten
- ¼ tsp hot sauce
- ½ cup buttermilk
- 3 tbsp light mayonnaise
- 3 tbsp chopped chives
- ⅛ tsp garlic powder
- ⅛ tsp onion powder
- Salt and pepper to taste

Directions:

1. Preheat air fryer to 350°F. Mix flour, cornmeal, Cajun seasoning, and parsley in a bowl. Put the beaten egg in a small bowl nearby. One at a time, dip a pickle slice in the egg, then roll in the crumb mixture. Gently press the crumbs, so they stick to the pickle. Place the chips in the greased frying basket and Air Fry for 7-9 minutes, flipping once until golden and crispy. In a bowl, whisk hot sauce, buttermilk, mayonnaise, chives, garlic and onion powder, salt, and pepper. Serve with pickles.

Cheese Straws

Servings: 8

Cooking Time: 7 Minutes

Ingredients:

- For dusting All-purpose flour
- Two quarters of one thawed sheet (that is, a half of the sheet cut into two even pieces; wrap and refreeze the remainder) A 17.25-ounce box frozen puff pastry
- 1 Large egg(s)
- 2 tablespoons Water
- ¼ cup (about ¾ ounce) Finely grated Parmesan cheese
- up to 1 teaspoon Ground black pepper

Directions:

1. Preheat the air fryer to 400°F.
2. Dust a clean, dry work surface with flour. Set one of the pieces of puff pastry on top, dust the pastry lightly with flour, and roll with a rolling pin to a 6-inch square.
3. Whisk the egg(s) and water in a small or medium bowl until uniform. Brush the pastry square(s) generously with this mixture. Sprinkle each square with 2 tablespoons grated cheese and up to ½ teaspoon ground black pepper.
4. Cut each square into 4 even strips. Grasp each end of 1 strip with clean, dry hands; twist it into a cheese straw. Place the twisted straws on a baking sheet.
5. Lay as many straws as will fit in the air-fryer basket—as a general rule, 4 of them in a small machine, 5 in a medium model, or 6 in a large. There should be space for air to circulate around the straws. Set the baking sheet with any remaining straws in the fridge.
6. Air-fry undisturbed for 7 minutes, or until puffed and crisp. Use tongs to transfer the cheese straws to a wire rack, then make subsequent batches in the same way (keeping the baking sheet with the remaining straws in the fridge as each batch cooks). Serve warm.

Roasted Red Pepper Dip

Servings: 2

Cooking Time: 15 Minutes

Ingredients:

- 2 Medium-size red bell pepper(s)
- 1¾ cups (one 15-ounce can) Canned white beans, drained and rinsed
- 1 tablespoon Fresh oregano leaves, packed
- 3 tablespoons Olive oil
- 1 tablespoon Lemon juice
- ½ teaspoon Table salt
- ½ teaspoon Ground black pepper

Directions:

1. Preheat the air fryer to 400°F.
2. Set the pepper(s) in the basket and air-fry undisturbed for 15 minutes, until blistered and even blackened.
3. Use kitchen tongs to transfer the pepper(s) to a zip-closed plastic bag or small bowl. Seal the bag or cover the bowl with plastic wrap. Set aside for 20 minutes.
4. Peel each pepper, then stem it, cut it in half, and remove all its seeds and their white membranes.
5. Set the pieces of the pepper in a food processor. Add the beans, oregano, olive oil, lemon juice, salt, and

pepper. Cover and process until smooth, stopping the machine at least once to scrape down the inside of the canister. Scrape the dip into a bowl and serve warm, or cover and refrigerate for up to 3 days (although the dip tastes best if it's allowed to come back to room temperature).

Sweet-and-salty Pretzels

Servings: 4

Cooking Time: 5 Minutes

Ingredients:

- 2 cups Plain pretzel nuggets
- 1 tablespoon Worcestershire sauce
- 2 teaspoons Granulated white sugar
- 1 teaspoon Mild smoked paprika
- ½ teaspoon Garlic or onion powder

Directions:

1. Preheat the air fryer to 350°F .
2. Put the pretzel nuggets, Worcestershire sauce, sugar, smoked paprika, and garlic or onion powder in a large bowl. Toss gently until the nuggets are well coated.
3. When the machine is at temperature, pour the nuggets into the basket, spreading them into as close to a single layer as possible. Air-fry, shaking the basket three or four times to rearrange the nuggets, for 5 minutes, or until the nuggets are toasted and aromatic. Although the coating will darken, don't let it burn, especially if the machine's temperature is 360°F.
4. Pour the nuggets onto a wire rack and gently spread them into one layer. (A rubber spatula does a good job.) Cool for 5 minutes before serving.

No-guilty Spring Rolls

Servings: 6

Cooking Time: 20 Minutes

Ingredients:

- 2 cups shiitake mushrooms, thinly sliced
- 4 cups green cabbage, shredded
- 4 tsp sesame oil
- 6 garlic cloves, minced
- 1 tbsp grated ginger
- 1 cup grated carrots
- Salt to taste
- 16 rice paper wraps
- ½ tsp ground cumin
- ½ tsp ground coriander

Directions:

1. Warm the sesame oil in a pan over medium heat. Add garlic, ginger, mushrooms, cabbage, carrots, cumin, coriander, and salt and stir-fry for 3-4 minutes or until the cabbage is wilted. Remove from heat. Get a piece of rice paper, wet with water, and lay it on a flat, non-absorbent surface. Place ¼ cup of the filling in the middle, then fold the bottom over the filling and fold the sides in. Roll up to make a mini burrito. Repeat until you have the number of spring rolls you want.
2. Preheat air fryer to 390°F. Place the spring rolls in the greased frying basket. Spray the tops with cooking oil and Air Fry for 8-10 minutes until golden. Serve immediately.

Asian Five-spice Wings

Servings: 4

Cooking Time: 15 Minutes

Ingredients:

- 2 pounds chicken wings
- ½ cup Asian-style salad dressing
- 2 tablespoons Chinese five-spice powder

Directions:

1. Cut off wing tips and discard or freeze for stock. Cut remaining wing pieces in two at the joint.
2. Place wing pieces in a large sealable plastic bag. Pour in the Asian dressing, seal bag, and massage the marinade into the wings until well coated. Refrigerate for at least an hour.
3. Remove wings from bag, drain off excess marinade, and place wings in air fryer basket.
4. Cook at 360°F for 15minutes or until juices run clear. About halfway through cooking time, shake the basket or stir wings for more even cooking.
5. Transfer cooked wings to plate in a single layer. Sprinkle half of the Chinese five-spice powder on the wings, turn, and sprinkle other side with remaining seasoning.

Stuffed Mushrooms

Servings: 10

Cooking Time: 8 Minutes

Ingredients:

- 8 ounces white mushroom caps, stems removed
- salt
- 6 fresh mozzarella cheese balls
- ground dried thyme
- ¼ roasted red pepper cut into small pieces (about ½ inch)

Directions:

1. Sprinkle inside of mushroom caps with salt to taste.
2. Cut mozzarella balls in half.

3. Stuff each cap with half a mozzarella cheese ball. Sprinkle very lightly with thyme.
4. Top each mushroom with a small strip of roasted red pepper, lightly pressing it into the cheese.
5. Cook at 390°F for 8minutes or longer if you prefer softer mushrooms.

Cuban Sliders

Servings: 8
Cooking Time: 8 Minutes

Ingredients:

- 8 slices ciabatta bread, ¼-inch thick
- cooking spray
- 1 tablespoon brown mustard
- 6-8 ounces thin sliced leftover roast pork
- 4 ounces thin deli turkey
- ⅓ cup bread and butter pickle slices
- 2–3 ounces Pepper Jack cheese slices

Directions:

1. Spray one side of each slice of bread with butter or olive oil cooking spray.
2. Spread brown mustard on other side of each slice.
3. Layer pork roast, turkey, pickles, and cheese on 4 of the slices. Top with remaining slices.
4. Cook at 390°F for approximately 8minutes. The sandwiches should be golden brown.
5. Cut each slider in half to make 8 portions.

Smoked Whitefish Spread

Servings: 1
Cooking Time: 10 Minutes

Ingredients:

- ¾ pound Boneless skinless white-flesh fish fillets, such as hake or trout
- 3 tablespoons Liquid smoke
- 3 tablespoons Regular, low-fat, or fat-free mayonnaise (gluten-free, if a concern)
- 2 teaspoons Jarred prepared white horseradish (optional)
- ¼ teaspoon Onion powder
- ¼ teaspoon Celery seeds
- ¼ teaspoon Table salt
- ¼ teaspoon Ground black pepper

Directions:

1. Put the fish fillets in a zip-closed bag, add the liquid smoke, and seal closed. Rub the liquid smoke all over the fish , then refrigerate the sealed bag for 2 hours.
2. Preheat the air fryer to 400°F.
3. Set a 12-inch piece of aluminum foil on your work surface. Remove the fish fillets from the bag and set them in the center of this piece of foil (the fillets can overlap). Fold the long sides of the foil together and crimp them closed. Make a tight seam so no steam can escape. Fold up the ends and crimp to seal well.
4. Set the packet in the basket and air-fry undisturbed for 10 minutes.
5. Use kitchen tongs to transfer the foil packet to a wire rack. Cool for a minute or so. Open the packet, transfer the fish to a plate, and refrigerate for 30 minutes.
6. Put the cold fish in a food processor. Add the mayonnaise, horseradish (if using), onion powder, celery seeds, salt, and pepper. Cover and pulse to a slightly coarse spread, certainly not fully smooth.
7. For a more traditional texture, put the fish fillets in a bowl, add the other ingredients, and stir with a wooden spoon, mashing the fish with everything else to make a coarse paste.
8. Scrape the spread into a bowl and serve at once, or cover with plastic wrap and store in the fridge for up to 4 days.

Greek Street Tacos

Servings: 8
Cooking Time: 3 Minutes

Ingredients:

- 8 small flour tortillas (4-inch diameter)
- 8 tablespoons hummus
- 4 tablespoons crumbled feta cheese
- 4 tablespoons chopped kalamata or other olives (optional)
- olive oil for misting

Directions:

1. Place 1 tablespoon of hummus or tapenade in the center of each tortilla. Top with 1 teaspoon of feta crumbles and 1 teaspoon of chopped olives, if using.
2. Using your finger or a small spoon, moisten the edges of the tortilla all around with water.
3. Fold tortilla over to make a half-moon shape. Press center gently. Then press the edges firmly to seal in the filling.
4. Mist both sides with olive oil.
5. Place in air fryer basket very close but try not to overlap.
6. Cook at 390°F for 3minutes, just until lightly browned and crispy.

Smoked Salmon Puffs

Servings: 2
Cooking Time: 8 Minutes
Ingredients:

- Two quarters of one thawed sheet (that is, a half of the sheet; wrap and refreeze the remainder) A 17.25-ounce box frozen puff pastry
- 4 1/2-ounce smoked salmon slices
- 2 tablespoons Softened regular or low-fat cream cheese (not fat-free)
- Up to 2 teaspoons Drained and rinsed capers, minced
- Up to 2 teaspoons Minced red onion
- 1 Large egg white
- 1 tablespoon Water

Directions:

1. Preheat the air fryer to 400°F.
2. For a small air fryer, roll the piece of puff pastry into a 6 x 6-inch square on a clean, dry work surface.
3. For a medium or larger air fryer, roll each piece of puff pastry into a 6 x 6-inch square.
4. Set 2 salmon slices on the diagonal, corner to corner, on each rolled-out sheet. Smear the salmon with cream cheese, then sprinkle with capers and red onion. Fold the sheet closed by picking up one corner that does not have an edge of salmon near it and folding the dough across the salmon to its opposite corner. Seal the edges closed by pressing the tines of a flatware fork into them.
5. Whisk the egg white and water in a small bowl until uniform. Brush this mixture over the top(s) of the packet(s).
6. Set the packet(s) in the basket (if you're working with more than one, they cannot touch). Air-fry undisturbed for 8 minutes, or until golden brown and flaky.
7. Use a nonstick-safe spatula to transfer the packet(s) to a wire rack. Cool for 5 minutes before serving.

Crab Toasts

Servings: 15
Cooking Time: 5 Minutes
Ingredients:

- 1 6-ounce can flaked crabmeat, well drained
- 3 tablespoons light mayonnaise
- 1/2 teaspoon lemon juice
- 1 teaspoon Worcestershire sauce
- 1/4 cup shredded sharp Cheddar cheese
- 1/4 cup shredded Parmesan cheese
- 1 loaf artisan bread, French bread, or baguette, cut into slices 3/8-inch thick

Directions:

1. Mix together all ingredients except the bread slices.
2. Spread each slice of bread with a thin layer of crabmeat mixture. (For a bread slice measuring 2 x 1 1/2 inches you will need about 1/2 tablespoon of crab mixture.)
3. Place in air fryer basket in single layer and cook at 360°F for 5minutes or until tops brown and toast is crispy.
4. Repeat step 3 to cook remaining crab toasts.

Roasted Chickpeas

Servings: 1
Cooking Time: 15 Minutes
Ingredients:

- 1 15-ounce can chickpeas, drained
- 2 teaspoons curry powder
- 1/4 teaspoon salt
- 1 tablespoon olive oil

Directions:

1. Drain chickpeas thoroughly and spread in a single layer on paper towels. Cover with another paper towel and press gently to remove extra moisture. Don't press too hard or you'll crush the chickpeas.
2. Mix curry powder and salt together.
3. Place chickpeas in a medium bowl and sprinkle with seasonings. Stir well to coat.
4. Add olive oil and stir again to distribute oil.
5. Cook at 390°F for 15minutes, stopping to shake basket about halfway through cooking time.
6. Cool completely and store in airtight container.

Poultry Recipes

Chicken Fried Steak With Gravy

Servings: 4
Cooking Time: 10 Minutes Per Batch
Ingredients:

- ½ cup flour
- 2 teaspoons salt, divided
- freshly ground black pepper
- ¼ teaspoon garlic powder
- 1 cup buttermilk
- 1 cup fine breadcrumbs
- 4 tenderized top round steaks (about 6 to 8 ounces each; ½-inch thick)
- vegetable or canola oil
- For the Gravy:
- 2 tablespoons butter or bacon drippings
- ¼ onion, minced (about ¼ cup)
- 1 clove garlic, smashed
- ¼ teaspoon dried thyme
- 3 tablespoons flour
- 1 cup milk
- salt and lots of freshly ground black pepper
- a few dashes of Worcestershire sauce

Directions:

1. Set up a dredging station. Combine the flour, 1 teaspoon of salt, black pepper and garlic powder in a shallow bowl. Pour the buttermilk into a second shallow bowl. Finally, put the breadcrumbs and 1 teaspoon of salt in a third shallow bowl.
2. Dip the tenderized steaks into the flour, then the buttermilk, and then the breadcrumb mixture, pressing the crumbs onto the steak. Place them on a baking sheet and spray both sides generously with vegetable or canola oil.
3. Preheat the air fryer to 400°F.
4. Transfer the steaks to the air fryer basket, two at a time, and air-fry for 10 minutes, flipping the steaks over halfway through the cooking time. This will cook your steaks to medium. If you want the steaks cooked a little more or less, add or subtract a minute or two. Hold the first batch of steaks warm in a 170°F oven while you cook the second batch.
5. While the steaks are cooking, make the gravy. Melt the butter in a small saucepan over medium heat on the stovetop. Add the onion, garlic and thyme and cook for five minutes, until the onion is soft and just starting to brown. Stir in the flour and cook for another five minutes, stirring regularly, until the mixture starts to brown. Whisk in the milk and bring the mixture to a boil to thicken. Season to taste with salt, lots of freshly ground black pepper and a few dashes of Worcestershire sauce.
6. Plate the chicken fried steaks with mashed potatoes and vegetables and serve the gravy at the table to pour over the top.

Coconut Chicken With Apricot-ginger Sauce

Servings: 4
Cooking Time: 8 Minutes Per Batch
Ingredients:

- 1½ pounds boneless, skinless chicken tenders, cut in large chunks (about 1¼ inches)
- salt and pepper
- ½ cup cornstarch
- 2 eggs
- 1 tablespoon milk
- 3 cups shredded coconut (see below)
- oil for misting or cooking spray
- Apricot-Ginger Sauce
- ½ cup apricot preserves
- 2 tablespoons white vinegar
- ¼ teaspoon ground ginger
- ¼ teaspoon low-sodium soy sauce
- 2 teaspoons white or yellow onion, grated or finely minced

Directions:

1. Mix all ingredients for the Apricot-Ginger Sauce well and let sit for flavors to blend while you cook the chicken.
2. Season chicken chunks with salt and pepper to taste.
3. Place cornstarch in a shallow dish.
4. In another shallow dish, beat together eggs and milk.
5. Place coconut in a third shallow dish. (If also using panko breadcrumbs, as suggested below, stir them to mix well.)
6. Spray air fryer basket with oil or cooking spray.
7. Dip each chicken chunk into cornstarch, shake off excess, and dip in egg mixture.

8. Shake off excess egg mixture and roll lightly in coconut or coconut mixture. Spray with oil.
9. Place coated chicken chunks in air fryer basket in a single layer, close together but without sides touching.
10. Cook at 360°F for 4minutes, stop, and turn chunks over.
11. Cook an additional 4 minutes or until chicken is done inside and coating is crispy brown.
12. Repeat steps 9 through 11 to cook remaining chicken chunks.

Quick Chicken For Filling

Servings: 2
Cooking Time: 8 Minutes
Ingredients:

- 1 pound chicken tenders, skinless and boneless
- ½ teaspoon ground cumin
- ½ teaspoon garlic powder
- cooking spray

Directions:

1. Sprinkle raw chicken tenders with seasonings.
2. Spray air fryer basket lightly with cooking spray to prevent sticking.
3. Place chicken in air fryer basket in single layer.
4. Cook at 390°F for 4minutes, turn chicken strips over, and cook for an additional 4minutes.
5. Test for doneness. Thick tenders may require an additional minute or two.

Mexican Chicken Roll-ups

Servings: 4
Cooking Time: 35 Minutes
Ingredients:

- ½ red bell pepper, cut into strips
- ½ green bell pepper, cut into strips
- 2 chicken breasts
- ½ lime, juiced
- 2 tbsp taco seasoning
- 1 spring onion, thinly sliced

Directions:

1. Preheat air fryer to 400°F. Cut the chicken into cutlets by slicing the chicken breast in half horizontally in order to have 4 thin cutlets. Drizzle with lime juice and season with taco seasoning. Divide the red pepper, green pepper, and spring onion equally between the 4 cutlets. Roll up the cutlets. Secure with toothpicks. Place the chicken roll-ups in the air fryer and lightly spray with cooking oil. Bake for 12 minutes, turning once. Serve warm.

Herb-marinated Chicken

Servings: 4
Cooking Time: 25 Minutes
Ingredients:

- 4 chicken breasts
- 2 tsp rosemary, minced
- 2 tsp thyme, minced
- Salt and pepper to taste
- ½ cup chopped cilantro
- 1 lime, juiced

Directions:

1. Place chicken in a resealable bag. Add rosemary, thyme, salt, pepper, cilantro, and lime juice. Seal the bag and toss to coat, then place in the refrigerator for 2 hours.
2. Preheat air fryer to 400°F. Arrange the chicken in a single layer in the greased frying basket. Spray the chicken with cooking oil. Air Fry for 6-7 minutes, then flip the chicken. Cook for another 3 minutes. Serve and enjoy!

Curried Chicken Legs

Servings:4
Cooking Time: 40 Minutes
Ingredients:

- ¾ cup Greek yogurt
- 1 tbsp tomato paste
- 2 tsp curry powder
- ½ tbsp oregano
- 1 tsp salt
- 1 ½ lb chicken legs
- 2 tbsp chopped fresh mint

Directions:

1. Combine yogurt, tomato paste, curry powder, oregano and salt in a bowl. Divide the mixture in half. Cover one half and store it in the fridge. Into the other half, toss in the chicken until coated and marinate covered in the fridge for 30 minutes up to overnight.
2. Preheat air fryer to 370°F. Shake excess marinade from chicken. Place chicken legs in the greased frying basket and Air Fry for 18 minutes, flipping once and brushing with yogurt mixture. Serve topped with mint.

Japanese-inspired Glazed Chicken

Servings: 4
Cooking Time: 25 Minutes

Ingredients:

- 4 chicken breasts
- Chicken seasoning to taste
- Salt and pepper to taste
- 2 tsp grated fresh ginger
- 2 garlic cloves, minced
- ¼ cup molasses
- 2 tbsp tamari sauce

Directions:

1. Preheat air fryer to 400°F. Season the chicken with seasoning, salt, and pepper. Place the chicken in the greased frying basket and Air Fry for 7 minutes, then flip the chicken. Cook for another 3 minutes.
2. While the chicken is cooking, combine ginger, garlic, molasses, and tamari sauce in a saucepan over medium heat. Cook for 4 minutes or until the sauce thickens. Transfer all of the chicken to a serving dish. Drizzle with ginger-tamari glaze and serve.

Chicken Nuggets

Servings: 20
Cooking Time: 14 Minutes Per Batch

Ingredients:

- 1 pound boneless, skinless chicken thighs, cut into 1-inch chunks
- ¾ teaspoon salt
- ½ teaspoon black pepper
- ½ teaspoon garlic powder
- ½ teaspoon onion powder
- ½ cup flour
- 2 eggs, beaten
- ½ cup panko breadcrumbs
- 3 tablespoons plain breadcrumbs
- oil for misting or cooking spray

Directions:

1. In the bowl of a food processor, combine chicken, ½ teaspoon salt, pepper, garlic powder, and onion powder. Process in short pulses until chicken is very finely chopped and well blended.
2. Place flour in one shallow dish and beaten eggs in another. In a third dish or plastic bag, mix together the panko crumbs, plain breadcrumbs, and ¼ teaspoon salt.
3. Shape chicken mixture into small nuggets. Dip nuggets in flour, then eggs, then panko crumb mixture.
4. Spray nuggets on both sides with oil or cooking spray and place in air fryer basket in a single layer, close but not overlapping.
5. Cook at 360°F for 10minutes. Spray with oil and cook 4 minutes, until chicken is done and coating is golden brown.
6. Repeat step 5 to cook remaining nuggets.

Windsor´s Chicken Salad

Servings:4
Cooking Time: 30 Minutes

Ingredients:

- ½ cup halved seedless red grapes
- 2 chicken breasts, cubed
- Salt and pepper to taste
- ¾ cup mayonnaise
- 1 tbsp lemon juice
- 2 tbsp chopped parsley
- ½ cup chopped celery
- 1 shallot, diced

Directions:

1. Preheat air fryer to 350ºF. Sprinkle chicken with salt and pepper. Place the chicken cubes in the frying basket and Air Fry for 9 minutes, flipping once. In a salad bowl, combine the cooked chicken, mayonnaise, lemon juice, parsley, grapes, celery, and shallot and let chill covered in the fridge for 1 hour up to overnight.

Parmesan Chicken Fingers

Servings: 2
Cooking Time: 19 Minutes

Ingredients:

- ½ cup flour
- 1 teaspoon salt
- freshly ground black pepper
- 2 eggs, beaten
- ¾ cup seasoned panko breadcrumbs
- ¾ cup grated Parmesan cheese
- 8 chicken tenders (about 1 pound)
- OR
- 2 to 3 boneless, skinless chicken breasts, cut into strips
- vegetable oil
- marinara sauce

Directions:

1. Set up a dredging station. Combine the flour, salt and pepper in a shallow dish. Place the beaten eggs in

second shallow dish, and combine the panko breadcrumbs and Parmesan cheese in a third shallow dish.
2. Dredge the chicken tenders in the flour mixture. Then dip them into the egg, and finally place the chicken in the breadcrumb mixture. Press the coating onto both sides of the chicken tenders. Place the coated chicken tenders on a baking sheet until they are all coated. Spray both sides of the chicken fingers with vegetable oil.
3. Preheat the air fryer to 360°F.
4. Air-fry the chicken fingers in two batches. Transfer half the chicken fingers to the air fryer basket and air-fry for 9 minutes, turning the chicken over halfway through the cooking time. When the second batch of chicken fingers has finished cooking, return the first batch to the air fryer with the second batch and air-fry for one minute to heat everything through.
5. Serve immediately with marinara sauce, honey-mustard, ketchup or your favorite dipping sauce.

Moroccan-style Chicken Strips

Servings: 4
Cooking Time: 30 Minutes
Ingredients:
- 4 chicken breasts, cut into strips
- 2 tsp olive oil
- 2 tbsp cornstarch
- 3 garlic cloves, minced
- ½ cup chicken broth
- ¼ cup lemon juice
- 1 tbsp honey
- ½ tsp ras el hanout
- 1 cup cooked couscous

Directions:
1. Preheat air fryer to 400°F. Mix the chicken and olive oil in a bowl, then add the cornstarch. Stir to coat. Add the garlic and transfer to a baking pan. Put the pan in the fryer. Bake for 10 minutes. Stir at least once during cooking.
2. When done, pour in the chicken broth, lemon juice, honey, and ras el hanout. Bake for an additional 6-9 minutes or until the sauce is thick and the chicken cooked through with no pink showing. Serve with couscous.

Garlic Chicken

Servings: 4
Cooking Time: 30 Minutes
Ingredients:
- 4 bone-in skinless chicken thighs
- 1 tbsp olive oil
- 1 tbsp lemon juice
- 3 tbsp cornstarch
- 1 tsp dried sage
- Black pepper to taste
- 20 garlic cloves, unpeeled

Directions:
1. Preheat air fryer to 370°F. Brush the chicken with olive oil and lemon juice, then drizzle cornstarch, sage, and pepper.Put the chicken in the frying basket and scatter the garlic cloves on top. Roast for 25 minutes or until the garlic is soft, and the chicken is cooked through. Serve.

Turkey Steaks With Green Salad

Servings: 4
Cooking Time: 20 Minutes
Ingredients:
- 1/3 cup shaved Parmesan cheese
- 3 tsp grated Parmesan cheese
- 4 turkey breast steaks
- Salt and pepper to taste
- 1 large egg, beaten
- ½ cup bread crumbs
- ½ tsp dried thyme
- 5 oz baby spinach
- 5 oz watercress
- 1 tbsp olive oil
- 1 tbsp lemon juice
- 2 spring onions, chopped
- 1 lemon, cut into wedges

Directions:
1. Place the steaks between two sheets of parchment paper. Pound the turkey to ¼-inch thick cutlets using a meat mallet or rolling pin. Season the cutlets with salt and pepper to taste. Put the beaten egg in a shallow bowl. Put the crumbs, thyme, and Parmesan in a second shallow bowl. Dip the cutlet in the egg bowl and then in the crumb mix. Press the crumbs so that they stick to the chicken. Preheat air fryer to 400°F. Fry the turkey in the greased frying basket for 8 minutes, flipping once until golden and cooked through. Repeat for all cutlets.
2. Put the spinach, spring onions, and watercress in a bowl. Toss with olive oil, lemon juice, salt, and pepper. Serve each cutlet on a plate topped with 1 ½ cups salad. Garnish with lemon wedges and shaved Parmesan cheese. Serve.

Chicken Strips

Servings: 4
Cooking Time: 8 Minutes
Ingredients:

- 1 pound chicken tenders
- Marinade
- ¼ cup olive oil
- 2 tablespoons water
- 2 tablespoons honey
- 2 tablespoons white vinegar
- ½ teaspoon salt
- ½ teaspoon crushed red pepper
- 1 teaspoon garlic powder
- 1 teaspoon onion powder
- ½ teaspoon paprika

Directions:

1. Combine all marinade ingredients and mix well.
2. Add chicken and stir to coat. Cover tightly and let marinate in refrigerator for 30minutes.
3. Remove tenders from marinade and place them in a single layer in the air fryer basket.
4. Cook at 390°F for 3minutes. Turn tenders over and cook for 5 minutes longer or until chicken is done and juices run clear.
5. Repeat step 4 to cook remaining tenders.

Katsu Chicken Thighs

Servings: 4
Cooking Time: 35 Minutes
Ingredients:

- 1 ½ lb boneless, skinless chicken thighs
- 3 tbsp tamari sauce
- 3 tbsp lemon juice
- ½ tsp ground ginger
- Black pepper to taste
- 6 tbsp cornstarch
- 1 cup chicken stock
- 2 tbsp hoisin sauce
- 2 tbsp light brown sugar
- 2 tbsp sesame seeds

Directions:

1. Preheat the air fryer to 400°F. After cubing the chicken thighs, put them in a cake pan. Add a tbsp of tamari sauce, a tbsp of lemon juice, ginger, and black pepper. Mix and let marinate for 10 minutes. Remove the chicken and coat it in 4 tbsp of cornstarch; set aside. Add the rest of the marinade to the pan and add the stock, hoisin sauce, brown sugar, and the remaining tamari sauce, lemon juice, and cornstarch. Mix well. Put the pan in the frying basket and Air Fry for 5-8 minutes or until bubbling and thick, stirring once. Remove and set aside.Put the chicken in the frying basket and Fry for 15-18 minutes, shaking the basket once. Remove the chicken to the sauce in the pan and return to the fryer to reheat for 2 minutes. Sprinkle with the sesame seeds and serve.

Teriyaki Chicken Legs

Servings: 2
Cooking Time: 20 Minutes
Ingredients:

- 4 tablespoons teriyaki sauce
- 1 tablespoon orange juice
- 1 teaspoon smoked paprika
- 4 chicken legs
- cooking spray

Directions:

1. Mix together the teriyaki sauce, orange juice, and smoked paprika. Brush on all sides of chicken legs.
2. Spray air fryer basket with nonstick cooking spray and place chicken in basket.
3. Cook at 360°F for 6minutes. Turn and baste with sauce. Cook for 6 moreminutes, turn and baste. Cook for 8 minutes more, until juices run clear when chicken is pierced with a fork.

Granny Pesto Chicken Caprese

Servings: 4
Cooking Time: 30 Minutes
Ingredients:

- 2 tbsp grated Parmesan cheese
- 4 oz fresh mozzarella cheese, thinly sliced
- 16 grape tomatoes, halved
- 4 garlic cloves, minced
- 1 tsp olive oil
- Salt and pepper to taste
- 4 chicken cutlets
- 1 tbsp prepared pesto
- 1 large egg, beaten
- ½ cup bread crumbs
- 2 tbsp Italian seasoning
- 1 tsp balsamic vinegar
- 2 tbsp chopped fresh basil

Directions:

1. Preheat air fryer to 400°F. In a bowl, coat the tomatoes with garlic, olive oil, salt and pepper. Air Fry for 5 minutes, shaking them twice. Set aside when soft.

2. Place the cutlets between two sheets of parchment paper. Pound the chicken to ¼-inch thickness using a meat mallet. Season on both sides with salt and pepper. Spread an even coat of pesto. Put the beaten egg in a shallow bowl. Mix the crumbs, Italian seasoning, and Parmesan in a second shallow bowl. Dip the chicken in the egg bowl, and then in the crumb mix. Press the crumbs so that they stick to the chicken.

3. Place the chicken in the greased frying basket. Air Fry the chicken for 6-8 minutes, flipping once until golden and cooked through. Put 1 oz of mozzarella and ¼ of the tomatoes on top of each cutlet. When all of the cutlets are cooked, return them to the frying basket and melt the cheese for 2 minutes. Remove from the fryer, drizzle with balsamic vinegar and basil on top.

Goat Cheese Stuffed Turkey Roulade

Servings: 4

Cooking Time: 55 Minutes

Ingredients:

- 1 boneless turkey breast, skinless
- Salt and pepper to taste
- 4 oz goat cheese
- 1 tbsp marjoram
- 1 tbsp sage
- 2 garlic cloves, minced
- 2 tbsp olive oil
- 2 tbsp chopped cilantro

Directions:

1. Preheat air fryer to 380°F. Butterfly the turkey breast with a sharp knife and season with salt and pepper. Mix together the goat cheese, marjoram, sage, and garlic in a bowl. Spread the cheese mixture over the turkey breast, then roll it up tightly, tucking the ends underneath.

2. Put the turkey breast roulade onto a piece of aluminum foil, wrap it up, and place it into the air fryer. Bake for 30 minutes. Turn the turkey breast, brush the top with oil, and then continue to cook for another 10-15 minutes. Slice and serve sprinkled with cilantro.

Enchilada Chicken Quesadillas

Servings: 4

Cooking Time: 35 Minutes

Ingredients:

- 2 cups cooked chicken breasts, shredded
- 1 can diced green chilies, including juice
- 2 cups grated Mexican cheese blend
- 3/4 cup sour cream
- 2 tsp chili powder
- 1 tsp cumin
- 1 tbsp chipotle sauce
- 1 tsp dried onion flakes
- ½ tsp salt
- 3 tbsp butter, melted
- 8 flour tortillas

Directions:

1. In a small bowl, whisk the sour cream, chipotle sauce and chili powder. Let chill in the fridge until ready to use.

2. Preheat air fryer at 350°F. Mix the chicken, green chilies, cumin, and salt in a bowl. Set aside. Brush on one side of a tortilla lightly with melted butter. Layer with ¼ cup of chicken, onion flakes and ¼ cup of Mexican cheese. Top with a second tortilla and lightly brush with butter on top. Repeat with the remaining ingredients. Place quesadillas, butter side down, in the frying basket and Bake for 3 minutes. Cut them into 6 sections and serve with cream sauce on the side.

Chicken Flautas

Servings: 6

Cooking Time: 8 Minutes

Ingredients:

- 6 tablespoons whipped cream cheese
- 1 cup shredded cooked chicken
- 6 tablespoons mild pico de gallo salsa
- ⅓ cup shredded Mexican cheese
- ½ teaspoon taco seasoning
- Six 8-inch flour tortillas
- 2 cups shredded lettuce
- ½ cup guacamole

Directions:

1. Preheat the air fryer to 370°F.

2. In a large bowl, mix the cream cheese, chicken, salsa, shredded cheese, and taco seasoning until well combined.

3. Lay the tortillas on a flat surface. Divide the cheese-and-chicken mixture into 6 equal portions; then place the mixture in the center of the tortillas, spreading evenly, leaving about 1 inch from the edge of the tortilla.

4. Spray the air fryer basket with olive oil spray. Roll up the flautas and place them edge side down into the basket. Lightly mist the top of the flautas with olive oil spray.

5. Repeat until the air fryer basket is full. You may need to cook these in batches, depending on the size of your air fryer.
6. Cook for 7 minutes, or until the outer edges are browned.
7. Remove from the air fryer basket and serve warm over a bed of shredded lettuce with guacamole on top.

Mushroom & Turkey Bread Pizza

Servings: 4
Cooking Time: 35 Minutes
Ingredients:

- 10 cooked turkey sausages, sliced
- 1 cup shredded mozzarella cheese
- 1 cup shredded Cheddar cheese
- 1 French loaf bread
- 2 tbsp butter, softened
- 1 tsp garlic powder
- 1 1/3 cups marinara sauce
- 1 tsp Italian seasoning
- 2 scallions, chopped
- 1 cup mushrooms, sliced

Directions:

1. Preheat the air fryer to 370°F. Cut the bread in half crosswise, then split each half horizontally. Combine butter and garlic powder, then spread on the cut sides of the bread. Bake the halves in the fryer for 3-5 minutes or until the leaves start to brown. Set the toasted bread on a work surface and spread marinara sauce over the top. Sprinkle the Italian seasoning, then top with sausages, scallions, mushrooms, and cheeses. Set the pizzas in the air fryer and Bake for 8-12 minutes or until the cheese is melted and starting to brown. Serve hot.

Chicago-style Turkey Meatballs

Servings: 6
Cooking Time: 15 Minutes
Ingredients:

- 1 lb ground turkey
- 1 tbsp orange juice
- Salt and pepper to taste
- ½ tsp smoked paprika
- ½ tsp chili powder
- 1 tsp cumin powder
- ¼ red bell pepper, diced
- 1 diced jalapeño pepper
- 2 garlic cloves, minced

Directions:

1. Preheat air fryer to 400°F. Combine all of the ingredients in a large bowl. Shape into meatballs. Transfer the meatballs into the greased frying basket. Air Fry for 4 minutes, then flip the meatballs. Air Fry for another 3 minutes until cooked through. Serve immediately.

Ranch Chicken Tortillas

Servings: 4
Cooking Time: 35 Minutes
Ingredients:

- 2 chicken breasts
- 1 tbsp Ranch seasoning
- 1 tbsp taco seasoning
- 1 cup flour
- 1 egg
- ½ cup bread crumbs
- 4 flour tortillas
- 1 ½ cups shredded lettuce
- 3 tbsp ranch dressing
- 2 tbsp cilantro, chopped

Directions:

1. Preheat air fryer to 370°F. Slice the chicken breasts into cutlets by cutting in half horizontally on a cutting board. Rub with ranch and taco seasonings. In one shallow bowl, add flour. In another shallow bowl, beat the egg. In the third shallow bowl, add bread crumbs.
2. Lightly spray the air fryer basket with cooking oil. First, dip the cutlet in the flour, dredge in egg, and then finish by coating with bread crumbs. Place the cutlets in the fryer and Bake for 6-8 minutes. Flip them and cook further for 4 minutes until crisp. Allow the chicken to cook for a few minutes, then cut into strips. Divide into 4 equal portions along with shredded lettuce, ranch dressing, cilantro and tortillas. Serve and enjoy!

Paprika Chicken Drumettes

Servings: 2
Cooking Time: 30 Minutes

Ingredients:

- 1 lb chicken drumettes
- 1 cup buttermilk
- 3/4 cup bread crumbs
- ½ tsp smoked paprika
- 1 tsp chicken seasoning
- ½ tsp garlic powder
- Salt and pepper to taste
- 3 tsp of lemon juice

Directions:

1. Mix drumettes and buttermilk in a bowl and let sit covered in the fridge overnight. Preheat air fryer at 350°F. In a shallow bowl, combine the remaining ingredients. Shake excess buttermilk off drumettes and dip them in the breadcrumb mixture. Place breaded drumettes in the greased frying basket and Air Fry for 12 minutes. Increase air fryer temperature to 400°F, toss chicken, and cook for 8 minutes. Let rest for 5 minutes before serving.

Chicken Tenders With Basil-strawberry Glaze

Servings:4
Cooking Time: 20 Minutes

Ingredients:

- 1 lb chicken tenderloins
- ¼ cup strawberry preserves
- 3 tbsp chopped basil
- 1 tsp orange juice
- ½ tsp orange zest
- Salt and pepper to taste

Directions:

1. Combine all ingredients, except for 1 tbsp of basil, in a bowl. Marinade in the fridge covered for 30 minutes.
2. Preheat air fryer to 350°F. Place the chicken tenders in the frying basket and Air Fry for 4-6 minutes. Shake gently the basket and turn over the chicken. Cook for 5 more minutes. Top with the remaining basil to serve.

Chicken Pigs In Blankets

Servings: 4
Cooking Time: 40 Minutes

Ingredients:

- 8 chicken drumsticks, boneless, skinless
- 2 tbsp light brown sugar
- 2 tbsp ketchup
- 1 tbsp grainy mustard
- 8 smoked bacon slices
- 1 tsp chopped fresh sage

Directions:

1. Preheat the air fryer to 350°F. Mix brown sugar, sage, ketchup, and mustard in a bowl and brush the chicken with it. Wrap slices of bacon around the drumsticks and brush with the remaining mix. Line the frying basket with round parchment paper with holes. Set 4 drumsticks on the paper, add a raised rack and set the other drumsticks on it. Bake for 25-35 minutes, moving the bottom drumsticks to the top, top to the bottom, and flipping at about 14-16 minutes. Sprinkle with sage and serve.

Chicken Cutlets With Broccoli Rabe And Roasted Peppers

Servings: 2
Cooking Time: 10 Minutes

Ingredients:

- ½ bunch broccoli rabe
- olive oil, in a spray bottle
- salt and freshly ground black pepper
- ⅔ cup roasted red pepper strips
- 2 (4-ounce) boneless, skinless chicken breasts
- 2 tablespoons all-purpose flour*
- 1 egg, beaten
- ⅓ cup seasoned breadcrumbs*
- 2 slices aged provolone cheese

Directions:

1. Bring a medium saucepot of salted water to a boil on the stovetop. Blanch the broccoli rabe for 3 minutes in the boiling water and then drain. When it has cooled a little, squeeze out as much water as possible, drizzle a little olive oil on top, season with salt and black pepper and set aside. Dry the roasted red peppers with a clean kitchen towel and set them aside as well.
2. Place each chicken breast between 2 pieces of plastic wrap. Use a meat pounder to flatten the chicken breasts to about ½-inch thick. Season the chicken on both sides with salt and pepper.
3. Preheat the air fryer to 400°F.
4. Set up a dredging station with three shallow dishes. Place the flour in one dish, the egg in a second dish and the breadcrumbs in a third dish. Coat the chicken on all sides with the flour. Shake off any excess flour and dip the chicken into the egg. Let the excess egg drip off

and coat both sides of the chicken in the breadcrumbs. Spray the chicken with olive oil on both sides and transfer to the air fryer basket.

5. Air-fry the chicken at 400°F for 5 minutes. Turn the chicken over and air-fry for another minute. Then, top the chicken breast with the broccoli rabe and roasted peppers. Place a slice of the provolone cheese on top and secure it with a toothpick or two.

6. Air-fry at 360° for 3 to 4 minutes to melt the cheese and warm everything together.

Asian-style Orange Chicken

Servings: 4
Cooking Time: 25 Minutes

Ingredients:

- 1 lb chicken breasts, cubed
- Salt and pepper to taste
- 6 tbsp cornstarch
- 1 cup orange juice
- ¼ cup orange marmalade
- ¼ cup ketchup
- ½ tsp ground ginger
- 2 tbsp soy sauce
- 1 1/3 cups edamame beans

Directions:

1. Preheat the air fryer to 375°F. Sprinkle the cubes with salt and pepper. Coat with 4 tbsp of cornstarch and set aside on a wire rack. Mix the orange juice, marmalade, ketchup, ginger, soy sauce, and the remaining cornstarch in a cake pan, then stir in the beans. Set the pan in the frying basket and Bake for 5-8 minutes, stirring once during cooking until the sauce is thick and bubbling. Remove from the fryer and set aside. Put the chicken in the frying basket and fry for 10-12 minutes, shaking the basket once. Stir the chicken into the sauce and beans in the pan. Return to the fryer and reheat for 2 minutes.

Parmesan Crusted Chicken Cordon Bleu

Servings: 2
Cooking Time: 14 Minutes

Ingredients:

- 2 (6-ounce) boneless, skinless chicken breasts
- salt and freshly ground black pepper
- 1 tablespoon Dijon mustard
- 4 slices Swiss cheese
- 4 slices deli-sliced ham
- ¼ cup all-purpose flour*
- 1 egg, beaten
- ¾ cup panko breadcrumbs*
- ⅓ cup grated Parmesan cheese
- olive oil, in a spray bottle

Directions:

1. Butterfly the chicken breasts. Place the chicken breast on a cutting board and press down on the breast with the palm of your hand. Slice into the long side of the chicken breast, parallel to the cutting board, but not all the way through to the other side. Open the chicken breast like a "book". Place a piece of plastic wrap over the chicken breast and gently pound it with a meat mallet to make it evenly thick.

2. Season the chicken with salt and pepper. Spread the Dijon mustard on the inside of each chicken breast. Layer one slice of cheese on top of the mustard, then top with the 2 slices of ham and the other slice of cheese.

3. Starting with the long edge of the chicken breast, roll the chicken up to the other side. Secure it shut with 1 or 2 toothpicks.

4. Preheat the air fryer to 350°F.

5. Set up a dredging station with three shallow dishes. Place the flour in the first dish. Place the beaten egg in the second shallow dish. Combine the panko breadcrumbs and Parmesan cheese together in the third shallow dish. Dip the stuffed and rolled chicken breasts in the flour, then the beaten egg and then roll in the breadcrumb-cheese mixture to cover on all sides. Press the crumbs onto the chicken breasts with your hands to make sure they are well adhered. Spray the chicken breasts with olive oil and transfer to the air fryer basket.

6. Air-fry at 350°F for 14 minutes, flipping the breasts over halfway through the cooking time. Let the chicken rest for a few minutes before removing the toothpicks, slicing and serving.

Taquitos

Servings: 12
Cooking Time: 6 Minutes Per Batch

Ingredients:

- 1 teaspoon butter
- 2 tablespoons chopped green onions
- 1 cup cooked chicken, shredded
- 2 tablespoons chopped green chiles
- 2 ounces Pepper Jack cheese, shredded
- 4 tablespoons salsa
- ½ teaspoon lime juice
- ¼ teaspoon cumin
- ½ teaspoon chile powder
- ⅛ teaspoon garlic powder
- 12 corn tortillas
- oil for misting or cooking spray

Directions:

1. Melt butter in a saucepan over medium heat. Add green onions and sauté a minute or two, until tender.
2. Remove from heat and stir in the chicken, green chiles, cheese, salsa, lime juice, and seasonings.
3. Preheat air fryer to 390°F.
4. To soften refrigerated tortillas, wrap in damp paper towels and microwave for 30 to 60 seconds, until slightly warmed.
5. Remove one tortilla at a time, keeping others covered with the damp paper towels. Place a heaping tablespoon of filling into tortilla, roll up and secure with toothpick. Spray all sides with oil or cooking spray.
6. Place taquitos in air fryer basket, either in a single layer or stacked. To stack, leave plenty of space between taquitos and alternate the direction of the layers, 4 on the bottom lengthwise, then 4 more on top crosswise.
7. Cook for 6minutes or until brown and crispy.
8. Repeat steps 6 and 7 to cook remaining taquitos.
9. Serve hot with guacamole, sour cream, salsa or all three!

Peanut Butter-barbeque Chicken

Servings: 4
Cooking Time: 20 Minutes

Ingredients:

- 1 pound boneless, skinless chicken thighs
- salt and pepper
- 1 large orange
- ½ cup barbeque sauce
- 2 tablespoons smooth peanut butter
- 2 tablespoons chopped peanuts for garnish (optional)
- cooking spray

Directions:

1. Season chicken with salt and pepper to taste. Place in a shallow dish or plastic bag.
2. Grate orange peel, squeeze orange and reserve 1 tablespoon of juice for the sauce.
3. Pour remaining juice over chicken and marinate for 30minutes.
4. Mix together the reserved 1 tablespoon of orange juice, barbeque sauce, peanut butter, and 1 teaspoon grated orange peel.
5. Place ¼ cup of sauce mixture in a small bowl for basting. Set remaining sauce aside to serve with cooked chicken.
6. Preheat air fryer to 360°F. Spray basket with nonstick cooking spray.
7. Remove chicken from marinade, letting excess drip off. Place in air fryer basket and cook for 5minutes. Turn chicken over and cook 5minutes longer.
8. Brush both sides of chicken lightly with sauce.
9. Cook chicken 5minutes, then turn thighs one more time, again brushing both sides lightly with sauce. Cook for 5 moreminutes or until chicken is done and juices run clear.
10. Serve chicken with remaining sauce on the side and garnish with chopped peanuts if you like.

Crispy Cordon Bleu

Servings: 4
Cooking Time: 25 Minutes

Ingredients:

- 4 deli ham slices, halved lengthwise
- 2 tbsp grated Parmesan
- 4 chicken breast halves
- Salt and pepper to taste
- 8 Swiss cheese slices
- 1 egg
- 2 egg whites
- ¾ cup bread crumbs
- 1 tsp garlic powder
- 1 tsp onion powder
- 1 tsp mustard powder

Directions:

1. Preheat air fryer to 400°F. Season the chicken cutlets with salt and pepper. On one cutlet, put a half slice of ham and cheese on the top. Roll the chicken

tightly, then set aside. Beat the eggs and egg whites in a shallow bowl. Put the crumbs, Parmesan, garlic, onion, and mustard powder, in a second bowl. Dip the cutlet in the egg bowl and then in the crumb mix. Press so that they stick to the chicken. Put the rolls of chicken seam side down in the greased frying basket and Air Fry for 12-14 minutes, flipping once until golden and cooked through. Serve.

Harissa Chicken Wings

Servings: 4

Cooking Time: 25 Minutes

Ingredients:

- 8 whole chicken wings
- 1 tsp garlic powder
- ¼ tsp dried oregano
- 1 tbsp harissa seasoning

Directions:

1. Preheat air fryer to 400°F. Season the wings with garlic, harissa seasoning, and oregano. Place them in the greased frying basket and spray with cooking oil spray. Air Fry for 10 minutes, shake the basket, and cook for another 5-7 minutes until golden and crispy. Serve warm.

Thai Turkey And Zucchini Meatballs

Servings: 4

Cooking Time: 12 Minutes

Ingredients:

- 1½ cups grated zucchini,
- squeezed dry in a clean kitchen towel (about 1 large zucchini)
- 3 scallions, finely chopped
- 2 cloves garlic, minced
- 1 tablespoon grated fresh ginger
- 1 tablespoon finely chopped fresh cilantro
- zest of 1 lime
- 1 teaspoon salt
- freshly ground black pepper
- 1½ pounds ground turkey (a mix of light and dark meat)
- 2 eggs, lightly beaten
- 1 cup Thai sweet chili sauce (spring roll sauce)
- lime wedges, for serving

Directions:

1. Combine the zucchini, scallions, garlic, ginger, cilantro, lime zest, salt, pepper, ground turkey and eggs in a bowl and mix the ingredients together. Gently shape the mixture into 24 balls, about the size of golf balls.
2. Preheat the air fryer to 380°F.
3. Working in batches, air-fry the meatballs for 12 minutes, turning the meatballs over halfway through the cooking time. As soon as the meatballs have finished cooking, toss them in a bowl with the Thai sweet chili sauce to coat.
4. Serve the meatballs over rice noodles or white rice with the remaining Thai sweet chili sauce and lime wedges to squeeze over the top.

Buttermilk-fried Drumsticks

Servings: 2

Cooking Time: 25 Minutes

Ingredients:

- 1 egg
- ½ cup buttermilk
- ¾ cup self-rising flour
- ¾ cup seasoned panko breadcrumbs
- 1 teaspoon salt
- ¼ teaspoon ground black pepper (to mix into coating)
- 4 chicken drumsticks, skin on
- oil for misting or cooking spray

Directions:

1. Beat together egg and buttermilk in shallow dish.
2. In a second shallow dish, combine the flour, panko crumbs, salt, and pepper.
3. Sprinkle chicken legs with additional salt and pepper to taste.
4. Dip legs in buttermilk mixture, then roll in panko mixture, pressing in crumbs to make coating stick. Mist with oil or cooking spray.
5. Spray air fryer basket with cooking spray.
6. Cook drumsticks at 360°F for 10minutes. Turn pieces over and cook an additional 10minutes.
7. Turn pieces to check for browning. If you have any white spots that haven't begun to brown, spritz them with oil or cooking spray. Continue cooking for 5 more minutes or until crust is golden brown and juices run clear. Larger, meatier drumsticks will take longer to cook than small ones.

Simple Buttermilk Fried Chicken

Servings: 4
Cooking Time: 27 Minutes

Ingredients:

- 1 (4-pound) chicken, cut into 8 pieces
- 2 cups buttermilk
- hot sauce (optional)
- 1½ cups flour*
- 2 teaspoons paprika
- 1 teaspoon salt
- freshly ground black pepper
- 2 eggs, lightly beaten
- vegetable oil, in a spray bottle

Directions:

1. Cut the chicken into 8 pieces and submerge them in the buttermilk and hot sauce, if using. A zipper-sealable plastic bag works well for this. Let the chicken soak in the buttermilk for at least one hour or even overnight in the refrigerator.
2. Set up a dredging station. Mix the flour, paprika, salt and black pepper in a clean zipper-sealable plastic bag. Whisk the eggs and place them in a shallow dish. Remove four pieces of chicken from the buttermilk and transfer them to the bag with the flour. Shake them around to coat on all sides. Remove the chicken from the flour, shaking off any excess flour, and dip them into the beaten egg. Return the chicken to the bag of seasoned flour and shake again. Set the coated chicken aside and repeat with the remaining four pieces of chicken.
3. Preheat the air fryer to 370°F.
4. Spray the chicken on all sides with the vegetable oil and then transfer one batch to the air fryer basket. Air-fry the chicken at 370°F for 20 minutes, flipping the pieces over halfway through the cooking process, taking care not to knock off the breading. Transfer the chicken to a plate, but do not cover. Repeat with the second batch of chicken.
5. Lower the temperature on the air fryer to 340°F. Flip the chicken back over and place the first batch of chicken on top of the second batch already in the basket. Air-fry for another 7 minutes and serve warm.

Spiced Chicken Breasts

Servings: 4
Cooking Time: 20 Minutes

Ingredients:

- ½ tsp dried oregano
- ½ tsp granulated garlic
- ½ tsp granulated onion
- ½ tsp chili powder
- ¼ tsp sweet paprika
- Salt and pepper to taste
- 1 lb chicken breasts, sliced
- 2 tbsp yellow mustard

Directions:

1. Preheat air fryer to 375°F. Mix together oregano, salt, garlic, onion, chili powder, paprika, and black pepper in a small bowl. Coat the chicken with mustard in a bowl. Sprinkle the seasoning mix over the chicken. Place the chicken in the greased frying basket and Air Fry for 7-8, flipping once until cooked through. Serve immediately.

Yummy Maple-mustard Chicken Kabobs

Servings:4
Cooking Time: 35 Minutes+ Chilling Time

Ingredients:

- 1 lb boneless, skinless chicken thighs, cubed
- 1 green bell pepper, chopped
- ½ cup honey mustard
- ½ yellow onion, chopped
- 8 cherry tomatoes
- 2 tbsp chopped scallions

Directions:

1. Toss chicken cubes and honey mustard in a bowl and let chill covered in the fridge for 30 minutes. Preheat air fryer to 350°F. Thread chicken cubes, onion, cherry tomatoes, and bell peppers, alternating, onto 8 skewers. Place them on a kebab rack. Place rack in the frying basket and Air Fry for 12 minutes. Top with scallions to serve.

Cheesy Chicken-avocado Paninis

Servings: 2
Cooking Time: 25 Minutes
Ingredients:

- 2 tbsp mayonnaise
- 4 tsp yellow mustard
- 4 sandwich bread slices
- 4 oz sliced deli chicken ham
- 2 oz sliced provolone cheese
- 2 oz sliced mozzarella
- 1 avocado, sliced
- 1 tomato, sliced
- Salt and pepper to taste
- 1 tsp sesame seeds
- 2 tbsp butter, melted

Directions:

1. Preheat air fryer at 350°F. Rub mayonnaise and mustard on the inside of each bread slice. Top 2 bread slices with chicken ham, provolone and mozzarella cheese, avocado, sesame seeds, and tomato slices. Season with salt and pepper. Then, close sandwiches with the remaining bread slices. Brush the top and bottom of each sandwich lightly with melted butter. Place sandwiches in the frying basket and Bake for 6 minutes, flipping once. Serve.

Beef , pork & Lamb Recipes

Pork Schnitzel With Dill Sauce

Servings: 4
Cooking Time: 4 Minutes
Ingredients:

- 6 boneless, center cut pork chops (about 1½ pounds)
- ½ cup flour
- 1½ teaspoons salt
- freshly ground black pepper
- 2 eggs
- ½ cup milk
- 1½ cups toasted fine breadcrumbs
- 1 teaspoon paprika
- 3 tablespoons butter, melted
- 2 tablespoons vegetable or olive oil
- lemon wedges
- Dill Sauce:
- 1 cup chicken stock
- 1½ tablespoons cornstarch
- ⅓ cup sour cream
- 1½ tablespoons chopped fresh dill
- salt and pepper

Directions:

1. Trim the excess fat from the pork chops and pound each chop with a meat mallet between two pieces of plastic wrap until they are ½-inch thick.
2. Set up a dredging station. Combine the flour, salt, and black pepper in a shallow dish. Whisk the eggs and milk together in a second shallow dish. Finally, combine the breadcrumbs and paprika in a third shallow dish.
3. Dip each flattened pork chop in the flour. Shake off the excess flour and dip each chop into the egg mixture. Finally dip them into the breadcrumbs and press the breadcrumbs onto the meat firmly. Place each finished chop on a baking sheet until they are all coated.
4. Preheat the air fryer to 400°F.
5. Combine the melted butter and the oil in a small bowl and lightly brush both sides of the coated pork chops. Do not brush the chops too heavily or the breading will not be as crispy.
6. Air-fry one schnitzel at a time for 4 minutes, turning it over halfway through the cooking time. Hold the cooked schnitzels warm on a baking pan in a 170°F oven while you finish air-frying the rest.
7. While the schnitzels are cooking, whisk the chicken stock and cornstarch together in a small saucepan over medium-high heat on the stovetop. Bring the mixture to a boil and simmer for 2 minutes. Remove the saucepan from heat and whisk in the sour cream. Add the chopped fresh dill and season with salt and pepper.
8. Transfer the pork schnitzel to a platter and serve with dill sauce and lemon wedges. For a traditional meal, serve this along side some egg noodles, spätzle or German potato salad.

Baharat Lamb Kebab With Mint Sauce

Servings: 6
Cooking Time: 50 Minutes
Ingredients:

- 1 lb ground lamb
- ¼ cup parsley, chopped
- 3 garlic cloves, minced
- 1 shallot, diced
- Salt and pepper to taste
- 1 tsp ground cumin
- ¼ tsp ground cinnamon
- ¼ tsp baharat seasoning
- ¼ tsp chili powder
- ¼ tsp ground ginger
- 3 tbsp olive oil
- 1 cup Greek yogurt
- ½ cup mint, chopped
- 2 tbsp lemon juice
- ¼ tsp hot paprika

Directions:

1. Preheat air fryer to 360°F. Mix the ground lamb, parsley, 2 garlic cloves, shallot, 2 tbsp olive oil, salt, black pepper, cumin, cinnamon, baharat seasoning, chili powder, and ginger in a bowl. Divide the mixture into 4 equal quantities, and roll each into a long oval. Drizzle with the remaining olive oil, place them in a single layer in the frying basket and Air Fry for 10 minutes. While the kofta is cooking, mix together the Greek yogurt, mint, remaining garlic, lemon juice, hot paprika, salt, and pepper in a bowl. Serve the kofta with mint sauce.

Beef Short Ribs

Servings: 4
Cooking Time: 20 Minutes
Ingredients:

- 2 tablespoons soy sauce
- 1 tablespoon sesame oil
- 2 tablespoons brown sugar
- 1 teaspoon ground ginger
- 2 garlic cloves, crushed
- 1 pound beef short ribs

Directions:

1. In a small bowl, mix together the soy sauce, sesame oil, brown sugar, and ginger. Transfer the mixture to a large resealable plastic bag, and place the garlic cloves and short ribs into the bag. Secure and place in the refrigerator for an hour (or overnight).
2. When you're ready to prepare the dish, preheat the air fryer to 330°F.
3. Liberally spray the air fryer basket with olive oil mist and set the beef short ribs in the basket.
4. Cook for 10 minutes, flip the short ribs, and then cook another 10 minutes.
5. Remove the short ribs from the air fryer basket, loosely cover with aluminum foil, and let them rest. The short ribs will continue to cook after they're removed from the basket. Check the internal temperature after 5 minutes to make sure it reached 145°F if you prefer a well-done meat. If it didn't reach 145°F and you would like it to be cooked longer, you can put it back into the air fryer basket at 330°F for another 3 minutes.
6. Remove from the basket and let it rest, covered with aluminum foil, for 5 minutes. Serve immediately.

Berbere Beef Steaks

Servings: 4
Cooking Time: 45 Minutes
Ingredients:

- 1 chipotle pepper in adobo sauce, minced
- 1 lb skirt steak
- 2 tbsp chipotle sauce
- ¼ tsp Berbere seasoning
- Salt and pepper to taste

Directions:

1. Cut the steak into 4 equal pieces, then place them on a plate. Mix together chipotle pepper, adobo sauce, salt, pepper, and Berbere seasoning in a bowl. Spread the mixture on both sides of the steak. Chill for 2 hours.
2. Preheat air fryer to 390°F. Place the steaks in the frying basket and Bake for 5 minutes on each side for well-done meat. Allow the steaks to rest for 5 more minutes. To serve, slice against the grain.

Corned Beef Hash

Servings: 6

Cooking Time: 15 Minutes

Ingredients:

- 3 cups (about 14 ounces) Frozen unseasoned hash brown cubes (no need to thaw)
- 9 ounces Deli corned beef, cut into ¾-inch-thick slices, then cubed
- ¾ cup Roughly chopped yellow or white onion
- ¾ cup Stemmed, cored, and roughly chopped red bell pepper
- 2½ tablespoons Olive oil
- ¼ teaspoon Dried thyme
- ¼ teaspoon Dried sage leaves
- Up to a ⅛ teaspoon Cayenne

Directions:

1. Preheat the air fryer to 400°F.
2. Mix all the ingredients in a large or very large bowl until the potato cubes and corned beef are coated in the spices.
3. Spread the mixture in the basket in as close to an even layer as you can. Air-fry for 15 minutes, tossing and rearranging the pieces at the 5- and 10-minute marks to expose covered bits, until the potatoes are browned, even crisp, and the mixture is very fragrant.
4. Pour the contents of the basket onto a serving platter or divide between serving plates. Cool for a couple of minutes before serving.

Meat Loaves

Servings: 4

Cooking Time: 19 Minutes

Ingredients:

- Sauce
- ¼ cup white vinegar
- ¼ cup brown sugar
- 2 tablespoons Worcestershire sauce
- ½ cup ketchup
- Meat Loaves
- 1 pound very lean ground beef
- ⅔ cup dry bread (approx. 1 slice torn into small pieces)
- 1 egg
- ⅓ cup minced onion
- 1 teaspoon salt
- 2 tablespoons ketchup

Directions:

1. In a small saucepan, combine all sauce ingredients and bring to a boil. Remove from heat and stir to ensure that brown sugar dissolves completely.
2. In a large bowl, combine the beef, bread, egg, onion, salt, and ketchup. Mix well.
3. Divide meat mixture into 4 portions and shape each into a thick, round patty. Patties will be about 3 to 3½ inches in diameter, and all four should fit easily into the air fryer basket at once.
4. Cook at 360°F for 18 minutes, until meat is well done. Baste tops of mini loaves with a small amount of sauce, and cook 1 minute.
5. Serve hot with additional sauce on the side.

Beef & Sauerkraut Spring Rolls

Servings: 4

Cooking Time: 20 Minutes

Ingredients:

- 5 Colby cheese slices, cut into strips
- 2 tbsp Thousand Island Dressing for dipping
- 10 spring roll wrappers
- 1/3 lb corned beef
- 2 cups sauerkraut
- 1 tsp ground cumin
- ½ tsp ground nutmeg
- 1 egg, beaten
- 1 tsp corn starch

Directions:

1. Preheat air fryer to 360°F. Mix the egg and cornstarch in a bowl to thicken. Lay out the spring roll wrappers on a clean surface. Place a few strips of the cut-up corned beef in the middle of the wraps. Sprinkle with Colby cheese, cumin, and nutmeg and top with 1-2 tablespoons of sauerkraut. Roll up and seal the seams with the egg and cornstarch mixture. Place the rolls in the greased frying basket. Bake for 7 minutes, shaking the basket several times until the spring rolls are golden brown. Serve warm with Thousand Island for dipping.

Argentinian Steak Asado Salad

Servings: 2

Cooking Time: 35 Minutes

Ingredients:

- 1 jalapeño pepper, sliced thin
- ¼ cup shredded pepper Jack cheese
- 1 avocado, peeled and pitted
- ¼ cup diced tomatoes
- ½ diced shallot
- 2 tsp chopped cilantro
- 2 tsp lime juice
- ½ lb flank steak
- 1 garlic clove, minced
- 1 tsp ground cumin
- Salt and pepper to taste
- ¼ lime
- 3 cups mesclun mix
- ½ cup pico de gallo

Directions:

1. Mash the avocado in a small bowl. Add tomatoes, shallot, cilantro, lime juice, salt, and pepper. Set aside. Season the steak with garlic, salt, pepper, and cumin.
2. Preheat air fryer to 400°F. Put the steak into the greased frying basket. Bake 8-10 minutes, flipping once until your desired doneness. Remove and let rest. Squeeze the lime over the steak and cut into thin slices. For one serving, plate half of mesclun, 2 tbsp of cheese, and ¼ cup guacamole. Place half of the steak slices on top t, then add ¼ cup pico de gallo and jalapeño if desired.

Double Cheese & Beef Burgers

Servings: 4

Cooking Time: 30 Minutes

Ingredients:

- 4 toasted onion buns, split
- ¼ cup breadcrumbs
- 2 tbsp milk
- 1 tp smoked paprika
- 6 tbsp salsa
- 2 tsp cayenne pepper
- 2 tbsp grated Cotija cheese
- 1 ¼ lb ground beef
- 4 Colby Jack cheese slices
- ¼ cup sour cream

Directions:

1. Preheat the air fryer to 375°F. Combine the breadcrumbs, milk, paprika, 2 tbsp of salsa, cayenne, and Cotija cheese in a bowl and mix. Let stand for 5 minutes. Add the ground beef and mix with your hands. Form into 4 patties and lay them on wax paper. Place the patties into the greased frying basket and Air Fry for 11-14 minutes, flipping once during cooking until golden and crunchy on the outside. Put a slice of Colby jack on top of each and cook for another minute until the cheese melts. Combine the remaining salsa with sour cream. Spread the mix on the bun bottoms, lay the patties on top, and spoon the rest of the mix over. Add the top buns and serve.

Balsamic Short Ribs

Servings: 2

Cooking Time: 30 Minutes

Ingredients:

- 1/8 tsp Worcestershire sauce
- ¼ cup olive oil
- ¼ cup balsamic vinegar
- ¼ cup chopped basil leaves
- ¼ cup chopped oregano
- 1 tbsp honey
- ¼ cup chopped fresh sage
- 3 cloves garlic, quartered
- ½ tsp salt
- 1 lb beef short ribs

Directions:

1. Add all ingredients, except for the short ribs, to a plastic resealable bag and shake to combine. Reserve 2 tbsp of balsamic mixture in a small bowl. Place short ribs in the plastic bag and massage into ribs. Seal the bag and let marinate in the fridge for 30 minutes up to overnight.
2. Preheat air fryer at 325°F. Place short ribs in the frying basket and Bake for 16 minutes, turn once and brush with extra sauce. Serve warm.

Spiced Beef Empanadas

Servings: 4
Cooking Time: 35 Minutes

Ingredients:

- 2 tbsp olive oil
- 6 oz ground beef
- 1 shallot, diced
- ½ tsp ground cumin
- ½ tsp nutmeg
- ½ tsp ground cloves
- 1 pinch of brown sugar
- 2 tsp red chili powder
- 4 empanada dough shells

Directions:

1. Preheat air fryer to 350°F. Warm the olive oil in a saucepan over medium heat. Crumble and cook the ground beef for 4-5 minutes. Add in the shallot, cumin, nutmeg, chili powder, and clove and stir-fry for 3 minutes. Kill the heat and let the mixture cool slightly. Divide the beef mixture between the empanada shells. Fold the empanada shells over and use a fork to seal the edges. Sprinkle brown sugar over. Place the empanadas in the foil-lined frying basket and Bake for 15 minutes. Halfway through, flip the empanadas. Cook them until golden. Serve and enjoy!

Apple Cornbread Stuffed Pork Loin With Apple Gravy

Servings: 4
Cooking Time: 61 Minutes

Ingredients:

- 4 strips of bacon, chopped
- 1 Granny Smith apple, peeled, cored and finely chopped
- 2 teaspoons fresh thyme leaves
- ¼ cup chopped fresh parsley
- 2 cups cubed cornbread
- ½ cup chicken stock
- salt and freshly ground black pepper
- 1 (2-pound) boneless pork loin
- kitchen twine
- Apple Gravy:
- 2 tablespoons butter
- 1 shallot, minced
- 1 Granny Smith apple, peeled, cored and finely chopped
- 3 sprigs fresh thyme
- 2 tablespoons flour
- 1 cup chicken stock
- ½ cup apple cider
- salt and freshly ground black pepper, to taste

Directions:

1. Preheat the air fryer to 400°F.
2. Add the bacon to the air fryer and air-fry for 6 minutes until crispy. While the bacon is cooking, combine the apple, fresh thyme, parsley and cornbread in a bowl and toss well. Moisten the mixture with the chicken stock and season to taste with salt and freshly ground black pepper. Add the cooked bacon to the mixture.
3. Butterfly the pork loin by holding it flat on the cutting board with one hand, while slicing into the pork loin parallel to the cutting board with the other. Slice into the longest side of the pork loin, but stop before you cut all the way through. You should then be able to open the pork loin up like a book, making it twice as wide as it was when you started. Season the inside of the pork with salt and freshly ground black pepper.
4. Spread the cornbread mixture onto the butterflied pork loin, leaving a one-inch border around the edge of the pork. Roll the pork loin up around the stuffing to enclose the stuffing, and tie the rolled pork in several places with kitchen twine or secure with toothpicks. Try to replace any stuffing that falls out of the roast as you roll it, by stuffing it into the ends of the rolled pork. Season the outside of the pork with salt and freshly ground black pepper.
5. Preheat the air fryer to 360°F.
6. Place the stuffed pork loin into the air fryer, seam side down. Air-fry the pork loin for 15 minutes at 360°F. Turn the pork loin over and air-fry for an additional 15 minutes. Turn the pork loin a quarter turn and air-fry for an additional 15 minutes. Turn the pork loin over again to expose the fourth side, and air-fry for an additional 10 minutes. The pork loin should register 155°F on an instant read thermometer when it is finished.
7. While the pork is cooking, make the apple gravy. Preheat a saucepan over medium heat on the stovetop and melt the butter. Add the shallot, apple and thyme sprigs and sauté until the apple starts to soften and brown a little. Add the flour and stir for a minute or two. Whisk in the stock and apple cider vigorously to prevent the flour from forming lumps. Bring the mixture to a boil to thicken and season to taste with salt and pepper.
8. Transfer the pork loin to a resting plate and loosely tent with foil, letting the pork rest for at least 5 minutes before slicing and serving with the apple gravy poured over the top.

Leftover Roast Beef Risotto

Servings: 4
Cooking Time: 30 Minutes
Ingredients:

- ½ chopped red bell pepper
- ½ chopped cooked roast beef
- 3 tbsp grated Parmesan
- 2 tsp butter, melted
- 1 shallot, finely chopped
- 3 garlic cloves, minced
- ¾ cup short-grain rice
- 1¼ cups beef broth

Directions:

1. Preheat air fryer to 390°F. Add the melted butter, shallot, garlic, and red bell pepper to a baking pan and stir to combine. Air Fry for 2 minutes, or until the vegetables are crisp-tender. Remove from the air fryer and stir in the rice, broth, and roast beef. Put the cooking pan back into the fryer and Bake for 18-22 minutes, stirring once during cooking until the rice is al dente and the beef is cooked through. Sprinkle with Parmesan and serve.

Classic Beef Meatballs

Servings: 4
Cooking Time: 30 Minutes
Ingredients:

- 3 tbsp buttermilk
- 1/3 cup bread crumbs
- 1 tbsp ketchup
- 1 egg
- ½ tsp dried marjoram
- Salt and pepper to taste
- 1 lb ground beef
- 20 Swiss cheese cubes

Directions:

1. Preheat air fryer to 390°F. Mix buttermilk, crumbs, ketchup, egg, marjoram, salt, and pepper in a bowl. Using your hands, mix in ground beef until just combined. Shape into 20 meatballs. Take one meatball and shape it around a Swiss cheese cube. Repeat this for the remaining meatballs. Lightly spray the meatballs with oil and place into the frying basket. Bake the meatballs for 10-13 minutes, turning once until they are cooked through. Serve and enjoy!

Lamb Chops In Currant Sauce

Servings: 4
Cooking Time: 30 Minutes
Ingredients:

- ½ cup chicken broth
- 2 tbsp red currant jelly
- 2 tbsp Dijon mustard
- 1 tbsp lemon juice
- ½ tsp dried thyme
- ½ tsp dried mint
- 8 lamb chops
- Salt and pepper to taste

Directions:

1. Preheat the air fryer to 375°F. Combine the broth, jelly, mustard, lemon juice, mint, and thyme and mix with a whisk until smooth. Sprinkle the chops with salt and pepper and brush with some of the broth mixture.
2. Set 4 chops in the frying basket in a single layer, then add a raised rack and lay the rest of the chops on top. Bake for 15-20 minutes. Then, lay them in a cake pan and add the chicken broth mix. Put in the fryer and Bake for 3-5 more minutes or until the sauce is bubbling and the chops are tender.

Stuffed Pork Chops

Servings: 4
Cooking Time: 12 Minutes
Ingredients:

- 4 boneless pork chops
- ½ teaspoon salt
- ½ teaspoon black pepper
- ¼ teaspoon paprika
- 1 cup frozen spinach, defrosted and squeezed dry
- 2 cloves garlic, minced
- 2 ounces cream cheese
- ¼ cup grated Parmesan cheese
- 1 tablespoon extra-virgin olive oil

Directions:

1. Pat the pork chops with a paper towel. Make a slit in the side of each pork chop to create a pouch.
2. Season the pork chops with the salt, pepper, and paprika.
3. In a small bowl, mix together the spinach, garlic, cream cheese, and Parmesan cheese.
4. Divide the mixture into fourths and stuff the pork chop pouches. Secure the pouches with toothpicks.
5. Preheat the air fryer to 400°F.
6. Place the stuffed pork chops in the air fryer basket and spray liberally with cooking spray. Cook for 6 minutes, flip and coat with more cooking spray, and cook another 6 minutes. Check to make sure the meat is cooked to an internal temperature of 145°F. Cook the pork chops in batches, as needed.

Lamb Chops

Servings: 2
Cooking Time: 20 Minutes

Ingredients:

- 2 teaspoons oil
- ½ teaspoon ground rosemary
- ½ teaspoon lemon juice
- 1 pound lamb chops, approximately 1-inch thick
- salt and pepper
- cooking spray

Directions:

1. Mix the oil, rosemary, and lemon juice together and rub into all sides of the lamb chops. Season to taste with salt and pepper.
2. For best flavor, cover lamb chops and allow them to rest in the fridge for 20 minutes.
3. Spray air fryer basket with nonstick spray and place lamb chops in it.
4. Cook at 360°F for approximately 20minutes. This will cook chops to medium. The meat will be juicy but have no remaining pink. Cook for a minute or two longer for well done chops. For rare chops, stop cooking after about 12minutes and check for doneness.

Tarragon Pork Tenderloin

Servings: 4
Cooking Time: 25 Minutes

Ingredients:

- ½ tsp dried tarragon
- 1 lb pork tenderloin, sliced
- Salt and pepper to taste
- 2 tbsp Dijon mustard
- 1 clove garlic, minced
- 1 cup bread crumbs
- 2 tbsp olive oil

Directions:

1. Preheat air fryer to 390°F. Using a rolling pin, pound the pork slices until they are about ¾ inch thick. Season both sides with salt and pepper. Coat the pork with mustard and season with garlic and tarragon. In a shallow bowl, mix bread crumbs and olive oil. Dredge the pork with the bread crumbs, pressing firmly, so that it adheres. Put the pork in the frying basket and Air Fry until the pork outside is brown and crisp, 12-14 minutes. Serve warm.

Barbecue-style London Broil

Servings: 5
Cooking Time: 17 Minutes

Ingredients:

- ¾ teaspoon Mild smoked paprika
- ¾ teaspoon Dried oregano
- ¾ teaspoon Table salt
- ¾ teaspoon Ground black pepper
- ¼ teaspoon Garlic powder
- ¼ teaspoon Onion powder
- 1½ pounds Beef London broil (in one piece)
- Olive oil spray

Directions:

1. Preheat the air fryer to 400°F.
2. Mix the smoked paprika, oregano, salt, pepper, garlic powder, and onion powder in a small bowl until uniform.
3. Pat and rub this mixture across all surfaces of the beef. Lightly coat the beef on all sides with olive oil spray.
4. When the machine is at temperature, lay the London broil flat in the basket and air-fry undisturbed for 8 minutes for the small batch, 10 minutes for the medium batch, or 12 minutes for the large batch for medium-rare, until an instant-read meat thermometer inserted into the center of the meat registers 130°F (not USDA-approved). Add 1, 2, or 3 minutes, respectively (based on the size of the cut) for medium, until an instant-read meat thermometer registers 135°F (not USDA-approved). Or add 3, 4, or 5 minutes respectively for medium, until an instant-read meat thermometer registers 145°F (USDA-approved).
5. Use kitchen tongs to transfer the London broil to a cutting board. Let the meat rest for 10 minutes. It needs a long time for the juices to be reincorporated into the meat's fibers. Carve it against the grain into very thin (less than ¼-inch-thick) slices to serve.

Barbecue-style Beef Cube Steak

Servings: 2
Cooking Time: 14 Minutes
Ingredients:

- 2 4-ounce beef cube steak(s)
- 2 cups (about 8 ounces) Fritos (original flavor) or a generic corn chip equivalent, crushed to crumbs (see here)
- 6 tablespoons Purchased smooth barbecue sauce, any flavor (gluten-free, if a concern)

Directions:

1. Preheat the air fryer to 375°F .
2. Spread the Fritos crumbs in a shallow soup plate or a small pie plate. Rub the barbecue sauce onto both sides of the steak(s). Dredge the steak(s) in the Fritos crumbs to coat well and thoroughly, turning several times and pressing down to get the little bits to adhere to the meat.
3. When the machine is at temperature, set the steak(s) in the basket. Leave as much air space between them as possible if you're working with more than one piece of beef. Air-fry undisturbed for 12 minutes, or until lightly brown and crunchy. If the machine is at 360°F, you may need to add 2 minutes to the cooking time.
4. Use kitchen tongs to transfer the steak(s) to a wire rack. Cool for 5 minutes before serving.

California Burritos

Servings: 4
Cooking Time: 17 Minutes
Ingredients:

- 1 pound sirloin steak, sliced thin
- 1 teaspoon dried oregano
- 1 teaspoon ground cumin
- ½ teaspoon garlic powder
- 16 tater tots
- ⅓ cup sour cream
- ½ lime, juiced
- 2 tablespoons hot sauce
- 1 large avocado, pitted
- 1 teaspoon salt, divided
- 4 large (8- to 10-inch) flour tortillas
- ½ cup shredded cheddar cheese or Monterey jack
- 2 tablespoons avocado oil

Directions:

1. Preheat the air fryer to 380°F.
2. Season the steak with oregano, cumin, and garlic powder. Place the steak on one side of the air fryer and the tater tots on the other side. (It's okay for them to touch, because the flavors will all come together in the burrito.) Cook for 8 minutes, toss, and cook an additional 4 to 6 minutes.
3. Meanwhile, in a small bowl, stir together the sour cream, lime juice, and hot sauce.
4. In another small bowl, mash together the avocado and season with ½ teaspoon of the salt, to taste.
5. To assemble the burrito, lay out the tortillas, equally divide the meat amongst the tortillas. Season the steak equally with the remaining ½ teaspoon salt. Then layer the mashed avocado and sour cream mixture on top. Top each tortilla with 4 tater tots and finish each with 2 tablespoons cheese. Roll up the sides and, while holding in the sides, roll up the burrito. Place the burritos in the air fryer basket and brush with avocado oil (working in batches as needed); cook for 3 minutes or until lightly golden on the outside.

Orange Glazed Pork Tenderloin

Servings: 3
Cooking Time: 23 Minutes
Ingredients:

- 2 tablespoons brown sugar
- 2 teaspoons cornstarch
- 2 teaspoons Dijon mustard
- ½ cup orange juice
- ½ teaspoon soy sauce*
- 2 teaspoons grated fresh ginger
- ¼ cup white wine
- zest of 1 orange
- 1 pound pork tenderloin
- salt and freshly ground black pepper
- oranges, halved (for garnish)
- fresh parsley or other green herb (for garnish)

Directions:

1. Combine the brown sugar, cornstarch, Dijon mustard, orange juice, soy sauce, ginger, white wine and orange zest in a small saucepan and bring the mixture to a boil on the stovetop. Lower the heat and simmer while you cook the pork tenderloin or until the sauce has thickened.
2. Preheat the air fryer to 370°F.
3. Season all sides of the pork tenderloin with salt and freshly ground black pepper. Transfer the tenderloin to the air fryer basket, bending the pork into a wide "U"

shape if necessary to fit in the basket. Air-fry at 370°F for 20 to 23 minutes, or until the internal temperature reaches 145°F. Flip the tenderloin over halfway through the cooking process and baste with the sauce.
4. Transfer the tenderloin to a cutting board and let it rest for 5 minutes. Slice the pork at a slight angle and serve immediately with orange halves and fresh herbs to dress it up. Drizzle any remaining glaze over the top.

Perfect Strip Steaks

Servings: 2
Cooking Time: 17 Minutes
Ingredients:

- 1½ tablespoons Olive oil
- 1½ tablespoons Minced garlic
- 2 teaspoons Ground black pepper
- 1 teaspoon Table salt
- 2 ¾-pound boneless beef strip steak(s)

Directions:

1. Preheat the air fryer to 375°F (or 380°F or 390°F, if one of these is the closest setting).
2. Mix the oil, garlic, pepper, and salt in a small bowl, then smear this mixture over both sides of the steak(s).
3. When the machine is at temperature, put the steak(s) in the basket with as much air space as possible between them for the larger batch. They should not overlap or even touch. That said, even just a ¼-inch between them will work. Air-fry for 12 minutes, turning once, until an instant-read meat thermometer inserted into the thickest part of a steak registers 127°F for rare (not USDA-approved). Or air-fry for 15 minutes, turning once, until an instant-read meat thermometer registers 145°F for medium (USDA-approved). If the machine is at 390°F, the steaks may cook 2 minutes more quickly than the stated timing.
4. Use kitchen tongs to transfer the steak(s) to a wire rack. Cool for 5 minutes before serving.

Honey Mesquite Pork Chops

Servings: 2
Cooking Time: 10 Minutes
Ingredients:

- 2 tablespoons mesquite seasoning
- ¼ cup honey
- 1 tablespoon olive oil
- 1 tablespoon water
- freshly ground black pepper
- 2 bone-in center cut pork chops (about 1 pound)

Directions:

1. Whisk the mesquite seasoning, honey, olive oil, water and freshly ground black pepper together in a shallow glass dish. Pierce the chops all over and on both sides with a fork or meat tenderizer. Add the pork chops to the marinade and massage the marinade into the chops. Cover and marinate for 30 minutes.
2. Preheat the air fryer to 330°F.
3. Transfer the pork chops to the air fryer basket and pour half of the marinade over the chops, reserving the remaining marinade. Air-fry the pork chops for 6 minutes. Flip the pork chops over and pour the remaining marinade on top. Air-fry for an additional 3 minutes at 330°F. Then, increase the air fryer temperature to 400°F and air-fry the pork chops for an additional minute.
4. Transfer the pork chops to a serving plate, and let them rest for 5 minutes before serving. If you'd like a sauce for these chops, pour the cooked marinade from the bottom of the air fryer over the top.

Beef & Barley Stuffed Bell Peppers

Servings: 4
Cooking Time: 30 Minutes
Ingredients:

- 1 cup pulled cooked roast beef
- 4 bell peppers, tops removed
- 1 onion, chopped
- ½ cup grated carrot
- 2 tsp olive oil
- 2 tomatoes, chopped
- 1 cup cooked barley
- 1 tsp dried marjoram

Directions:

1. Preheat air fryer to 400°F. Cut the tops of the bell peppers, then remove the stems. Put the onion, carrots, and olive oil in a baking pan and cook for 2-4 minutes. The veggies should be crispy but soft. Put the veggies in a bowl, toss in the tomatoes, barley, roast beef, and marjoram, and mix to combine. Spoon the veggie mix into the cleaned bell peppers and put them in the frying basket. Bake for 12-16 minutes or until the peppers are tender. Serve warm.

Beefy Quesadillas

Servings: 4
Cooking Time: 45 Minutes
Ingredients:

- 2 cups grated cheddar
- 1 tsp chili powder
- ½ tsp smoked paprika
- ½ tsp ground cumin
- ½ tsp nutmeg
- ¼ tsp garlic powder
- Salt and pepper to taste
- 1 ribeye steak
- 2 tsp olive oil
- 1 red bell pepper, diced
- 1 grated carrot
- 1 green bell pepper, diced
- ½ red onion, sliced
- 1 cup corn kernels
- 3 tbsp butter, melted
- 8 tortillas

Directions:

1. Mix the chili powder, nutmeg, paprika, cumin, garlic powder, salt, and pepper in a bowl. Toss in ribeye until fully coated and let marinate covered in the fridge for 30 minutes. Preheat air fryer at 400°F. Place ribeye in the greased frying basket and Bake for 6 minutes until rare, flipping once. Let rest onto a cutting board for 5 minutes before slicing thinly against the grain.
2. Warm the olive oil in a skillet over high heat. Add in bell peppers, carrot and onion and cook for 6-8 minutes until the peppers are tender. Stir in corn. Set aside. Preheat air fryer at 350°F. Brush on one side of a tortilla lightly with melted butter. Layer ¼ beef strips, ¼ bell pepper mixture, and finally, ¼ of the grated cheese. Top with a second tortilla and lightly brush with butter on top. Repeat with the remaining ingredients. Place quesadillas, butter side down, in the frying basket and Bake for 3 minutes. Cut them into 6 sections and serve.

Pork Loin

Servings: 8
Cooking Time: 50 Minutes
Ingredients:

- 1 tablespoon lime juice
- 1 tablespoon orange marmalade
- 1 teaspoon coarse brown mustard
- 1 teaspoon curry powder
- 1 teaspoon dried lemongrass
- 2-pound boneless pork loin roast
- salt and pepper
- cooking spray

Directions:

1. Mix together the lime juice, marmalade, mustard, curry powder, and lemongrass.
2. Rub mixture all over the surface of the pork loin. Season to taste with salt and pepper.
3. Spray air fryer basket with nonstick spray and place pork roast diagonally in basket.
4. Cook at 360°F for approximately 50 minutes, until roast registers 130°F on a meat thermometer.
5. Wrap roast in foil and let rest for 10minutes before slicing.

Traditional Moo Shu Pork Lettuce Wraps

Servings: 4
Cooking Time: 40 Minutes
Ingredients:

- ½ cup sliced shiitake mushrooms
- 1 lb boneless pork loin, cubed
- 3 tbsp cornstarch
- 2 tbsp rice vinegar
- 3 tbsp hoisin sauce
- 1 tsp oyster sauce
- 3 tsp sesame oil
- 1 tsp sesame seeds
- ¼ tsp ground ginger
- 1 egg
- 2 tbsp flour
- 1 bag coleslaw mix
- 1 cup chopped baby spinach
- 3 green onions, sliced
- 8 iceberg lettuce leaves

Directions:

1. Preheat air fryer at 350°F. Make a slurry by whisking 1 tbsp of cornstarch and 1 tbsp of water in a bowl. Set aside. Warm a saucepan over heat, add in rice vinegar, hoisin sauce, oyster sauce, 1 tsp of sesame oil, and ginger, and cook for 3 minutes, stirring often. Add in cornstarch slurry and cook for 1 minute. Set aside and let the mixture thicken. Beat the egg, flour, and the remaining cornstarch in a bowl. Set aside.
2. Dredge pork cubes in the egg mixture. Shake off any excess. Place them in the greased frying basket and Air Fry for 8 minutes, shaking once. Warm the

remaining sesame oil in a skillet over medium heat. Add in coleslaw mix, baby spinach, green onions, and mushrooms and cook for 5 minutes until the coleslaw wilts. Turn the heat off. Add in cooked pork, pour in oyster sauce mixture, and toss until coated. Divide mixture between lettuce leaves, sprinkle with sesame seed, roll them up, and serve.

Crispy Ham And Eggs

Servings: 3

Cooking Time: 9 Minutes

Ingredients:

- 2 cups Rice-puff cereal, such as Rice Krispies
- ¼ cup Maple syrup
- ½ pound ¼- to ½-inch-thick ham steak (gluten-free, if a concern)
- 1 tablespoon Unsalted butter
- 3 Large eggs
- ⅛ teaspoon Table salt
- ⅛ teaspoon Ground black pepper

Directions:

1. Preheat the air fryer to 400°F.
2. Pour the cereal into a food processor, cover, and process until finely ground. Pour the ground cereal into a shallow soup plate or a small pie plate.
3. Smear the maple syrup on both sides of the ham, then set the ham into the ground cereal. Turn a few times, pressing gently, until evenly coated.
4. Set the ham steak in the basket and air-fry undisturbed for 5 minutes, or until browned.
5. Meanwhile, melt the butter in a medium or large nonstick skillet set over medium heat. Crack the eggs into the skillet and cook until the whites are set and the yolks are hot, about 3 minutes (or 4 minutes for a more set yolk.) Season with the salt and pepper.
6. When the ham is ready, transfer it to a serving platter, then slip the eggs from the skillet on top of it. Divide into portions to serve.

Garlic And Oregano Lamb Chops

Servings: 4

Cooking Time: 17 Minutes

Ingredients:

- 1½ tablespoons Olive oil
- 1 tablespoon Minced garlic
- 1 teaspoon Dried oregano
- 1 teaspoon Finely minced orange zest
- ¾ teaspoon Fennel seeds
- ¾ teaspoon Table salt
- ¾ teaspoon Ground black pepper
- 6 4-ounce, 1-inch-thick lamb loin chops

Directions:

1. Mix the olive oil, garlic, oregano, orange zest, fennel seeds, salt, and pepper in a large bowl. Add the chops and toss well to coat. Set aside as the air fryer heats, tossing one more time.
2. Preheat the air fryer to 400°F.
3. Set the chops bone side down in the basket (that is, so they stand up on their bony edge) with as much air space between them as possible. Air-fry undisturbed for 14 minutes for medium-rare, or until an instant-read meat thermometer inserted into the thickest part of a chop (without touching bone) registers 132°F (not USDA-approved). Or air-fry undisturbed for 17 minutes for well done, or until an instant-read meat thermometer registers 145°F (USDA-approved).
4. Use kitchen tongs to transfer the chops to a wire rack. Cool for 5 minutes before serving.

Sirloin Steak Bites With Gravy

Servings: 4

Cooking Time: 20 Minutes

Ingredients:

- 1 ½ lb sirloin steak, cubed
- 1 tbsp olive oil
- 2 tbsp cornstarch, divided
- 2 tbsp soy sauce
- 2 tbsp Worcestershire sauce
- 2 garlic cloves, minced
- Salt and pepper to taste
- ½ tsp smoked paprika
- ½ cup sliced red onion
- 2 fresh thyme sprigs
- ½ cup sliced mushrooms
- 1 cup beef broth
- 1 tbsp butter

Directions:

1. Preheat air fryer to 400°F. Combine beef, olive oil, 1 tablespoon of cornstarch, garlic, pepper, Worcestershire sauce, soy sauce, thyme, salt, and paprika. Arrange the beef on the greased baking dish, then top with onions and mushrooms. Place the dish in the frying basket and bake for 4 minutes. While the beef is baking, whisk beef broth and the rest of the cornstarch in a small bowl. When the beef is ready, add butter and beef broth to the baking dish. Bake for

another 5 minutes. Allow resting for 5 minutes. Serve and enjoy.

Friday Night Cheeseburgers

Servings: 4
Cooking Time: 20 Minutes
Ingredients:

- 1 lb ground beef
- 1 tsp Worcestershire sauce
- 1 tbsp allspice
- Salt and pepper to taste
- 4 cheddar cheese slices
- 4 buns

Directions:

1. Preheat air fryer to 360°F. Combine beef, Worcestershire sauce, allspice, salt and pepper in a large bowl. Divide into 4 equal portions and shape into patties. Place the burgers in the greased frying basket and Air Fry for 8 minutes. Flip and cook for another 3-4 minutes. Top each burger with cheddar cheese and cook for another minute so the cheese melts. Transfer to a bun and serve.

Air-fried Roast Beef With Rosemary Roasted Potatoes

Servings: 8
Cooking Time: 60 Minutes
Ingredients:

- 1 (5-pound) top sirloin roast
- salt and freshly ground black pepper
- 1 teaspoon dried thyme
- 2 pounds red potatoes, halved or quartered
- 2 teaspoons olive oil
- 1 teaspoon very finely chopped fresh rosemary, plus more for garnish

Directions:

1. Start by making sure your roast will fit into the air fryer basket without touching the top element. Trim it if you have to in order to get it to fit nicely in your air fryer. (You can always save the trimmings for another use, like a beef sandwich.)
2. Preheat the air fryer to 360°F.
3. Season the beef all over with salt, pepper and thyme. Transfer the seasoned roast to the air fryer basket.
4. Air-fry at 360°F for 20 minutes. Turn the roast over and continue to air-fry at 360°F for another 20 minutes.
5. Toss the potatoes with the olive oil, salt, pepper and fresh rosemary. Turn the roast over again in the air fryer basket and toss the potatoes in around the sides of the roast. Air-fry the roast and potatoes at 360°F for another 20 minutes. Check the internal temperature of the roast with an instant-read thermometer, and continue to roast until the beef is 5° lower than your desired degree of doneness. (Rare – 130°F, Medium – 150°F, Well done – 170°F.) Let the roast rest for 5 to 10 minutes before slicing and serving. While the roast is resting, continue to air-fry the potatoes if desired for extra browning and crispiness.
6. Slice the roast and serve with the potatoes, adding a little more fresh rosemary if desired.

Sage Pork With Potatoes

Servings: 4
Cooking Time: 30 Minutes
Ingredients:

- 2 cups potatoes
- 2 tsp olive oil
- 1 lb pork tenderloin, cubed
- 1 onion, chopped
- 1 red bell pepper, chopped
- 2 garlic cloves, minced
- ½ tsp dried sage
- ½ tsp fennel seeds, crushed
- 2 tbsp chicken broth

Directions:

1. Preheat air fryer to 370°F. Add the potatoes and olive oil to a bowl and toss to coat. Transfer them to the frying basket and Air Fry for 15 minutes. Remove the bowl. Add the pork, onion, red bell pepper, garlic, sage, and fennel seeds, to the potatoes, add chicken broth and stir gently. Return the bowl to the frying basket and cook for 10 minutes. Be sure to shake the basket at least once. The pork should be cooked through and the potatoes soft and crispy. Serve immediately.

Original Köttbullar

Servings: 4
Cooking Time: 30 Minutes
Ingredients:

- 1 lb ground beef
- 1 small onion, chopped
- 1 clove garlic, minced
- 1/3 cup bread crumbs
- 1 egg, beaten
- Salt and pepper to taste
- 1 cup beef broth
- 1/3 cup heavy cream
- 2 tbsp flour

Directions:

1. Preheat air fryer to 370°F. Combine beef, onion, garlic, crumbs, egg, salt and pepper in a bowl. Scoop 2 tbsp of mixture and form meatballs with hands. Place the meatballs in the greased frying basket. Bake for 14 minutes.
2. Meanwhile, stir-fry beef broth and heavy cream in a saucepan over medium heat for 2 minutes; stir in flour. Cover and simmer for 4 minutes or until the sauce thicken. Transfer meatballs to a serving dish and drizzle with sauce. Serve and enjoy!

Spanish-style Meatloaf With Manzanilla Olives

Servings: 6
Cooking Time: 35 Minutes
Ingredients:

- 2 oz Manchego cheese, grated
- 1 lb lean ground beef
- 2 eggs
- 2 tomatoes, diced
- ½ white onion, diced
- ½ cup bread crumbs
- 1 tsp garlic powder
- 1 tsp dried oregano
- 1 tsp dried thyme
- Salt and pepper to taste
- 4 Manzanilla olives, minced
- 1 tbsp olive oil
- 2 tbsp chopped parsley

Directions:

1. Preheat the oven to 380°F. Combine the ground beef, eggs, tomatoes, onion, bread crumbs, garlic powder, oregano, thyme, salt, pepper, olives and cheese in a bowl and mix well. Form into a loaf, flattening to 1-inch thick. Lightly brush the top with olive oil, then place the meatloaf into the frying basket. Bake for 25 minutes. Allow to rest for 5 minutes. Top with parsley and slice. Serve warm.

Tuscan Veal Chops

Servings: 2
Cooking Time: 12-15 Minutes
Ingredients:

- 4 teaspoons Olive oil
- 2 teaspoons Finely minced garlic
- 2 teaspoons Finely minced fresh rosemary leaves
- 1 teaspoon Finely grated lemon zest
- 1 teaspoon Crushed fennel seeds
- 1 teaspoon Table salt
- Up to ¼ teaspoon Red pepper flakes
- 2 10-ounce bone-in veal loin or rib chop(s), about ½ inch thick

Directions:

1. Preheat the air fryer to 400°F.
2. Mix the oil, garlic, rosemary, lemon zest, fennel seeds, salt, and red pepper flakes in a small bowl. Rub this mixture onto both sides of the veal chop(s). Set aside at room temperature as the machine comes to temperature.
3. Set the chop(s) in the basket. If you're cooking more than one chop, leave as much air space between them as possible. Air-fry undisturbed for 12 minutes for medium-rare, or until an instant-read meat thermometer inserted into the center of a chop (without touching bone) registers 135°F (not USDA-approved). Or air-fry undisturbed for 15 minutes for medium-well, or until an instant-read meat thermometer registers 145°F (USDA-approved).
4. Use kitchen tongs to transfer the chops to a cutting board or a wire rack. Cool for 5 minutes before serving.

Beef And Spinach Braciole

Servings: 4
Cooking Time: 92 Minutes
Ingredients:

- 7-inch oven-safe baking pan or casserole
- ½ onion, finely chopped
- 1 teaspoon olive oil
- ⅓ cup red wine
- 2 cups crushed tomatoes
- 1 teaspoon Italian seasoning
- ½ teaspoon garlic powder
- ¼ teaspoon crushed red pepper flakes
- 2 tablespoons chopped fresh parsley
- 2 top round steaks (about 1½ pounds)
- salt and freshly ground black pepper
- 2 cups fresh spinach, chopped
- 1 clove minced garlic
- ½ cup roasted red peppers, julienned
- ½ cup grated pecorino cheese
- ¼ cup pine nuts, toasted and rough chopped
- 2 tablespoons olive oil

Directions:

1. Preheat the air fryer to 400°F.
2. Toss the onions and olive oil together in a 7-inch metal baking pan or casserole dish. Air-fry at 400°F for 5 minutes, stirring a couple times during the cooking process. Add the red wine, crushed tomatoes, Italian seasoning, garlic powder, red pepper flakes and parsley and stir. Cover the pan tightly with aluminum foil, lower the air fryer temperature to 350°F and continue to air-fry for 15 minutes.
3. While the sauce is simmering, prepare the beef. Using a meat mallet, pound the beef until it is ¼-inch thick. Season both sides of the beef with salt and pepper. Combine the spinach, garlic, red peppers, pecorino cheese, pine nuts and olive oil in a medium bowl. Season with salt and freshly ground black pepper. Spread the mixture evenly over the steaks. Starting at one of the short ends, roll the beef around the filling, tucking in the sides as you roll to ensure the filling is completely enclosed. Secure the beef rolls with toothpicks.
4. Remove the baking pan with the sauce from the air fryer and set it aside. Preheat the air fryer to 400°F.
5. Brush or spray the beef rolls with a little olive oil and air-fry at 400°F for 12 minutes, rotating the beef during the cooking process for even browning. When the beef is browned, submerge the rolls into the sauce in the baking pan, cover the pan with foil and return it to the air fryer. Air-fry at 250°F for 60 minutes.
6. Remove the beef rolls from the sauce. Cut each roll into slices and serve with pasta, ladling some of the sauce overtop.

Fish And Seafood Recipes

Fried Scallops

Servings:3
Cooking Time: 6 Minutes
Ingredients:

- ½ cup All-purpose flour or tapioca flour
- 1 Large egg(s), well beaten
- 2 cups Corn flake crumbs (gluten-free, if a concern)
- Up to 2 teaspoons Cayenne
- 1 teaspoon Celery seeds
- 1 teaspoon Table salt
- 1 pound Sea scallops
- Vegetable oil spray

Directions:

1. Preheat the air fryer to 400°F.
2. Set up and fill three shallow soup plates or small pie plates on your counter: one for the flour; one for the beaten egg(s); and one for the corn flake crumbs, stirred with the cayenne, celery seeds, and salt until well combined.
3. One by one, dip a scallop in the flour, turning it every way to coat it thoroughly. Gently shake off any excess flour, then dip the scallop in the egg(s), turning it again to coat all sides. Let any excess egg slip back into the rest, then set the scallop in the corn flake mixture. Turn it several times, pressing gently to get an even coating on the scallop all around. Generously coat the scallop with vegetable oil spray, then set it aside on

a cutting board. Coat the remaining scallops in the same way.

4. Set the scallops in the basket with as much air space between them as possible. They should not touch. Air-fry undisturbed for 6 minutes, or until lightly browned and firm.

5. Use kitchen tongs to gently transfer the scallops to a wire rack. Cool for only a minute or two before serving.

Old Bay Crab Cake Burgers

Servings: 4

Cooking Time: 30 Minutes

Ingredients:

- ½ cup panko bread crumbs
- 1 egg, beaten
- 1 tbsp hummus
- 1 tsp Dijon mustard
- ¼ cup minced parsley
- 2 spring onions, chopped
- ½ tsp red chili powder
- 1 tbsp lemon juice
- ½ tsp Old Bay seasoning
- ⅛ tsp sweet paprika
- Salt and pepper to taste
- 10 oz lump crabmeat
- ¼ cup mayonnaise
- 2 tbsp minced dill pickle
- 1 tsp fresh lemon juice
- ¾ tsp Cajun seasoning
- 4 Boston lettuce leaves
- 4 buns, split

Directions:

1. Mix the crumbs, egg, hummus, mustard, parsley, lemon juice, red chili, spring onions, Old Bay seasoning, paprika, salt, and pepper in a large bowl. Fold in crabmeat until just coated without overmixing. Divide into 4 equal parts, about ½ cup each, and shape into patties, about ¾-inch thick. Preheat air fryer to 400°F.
2. Place the cakes in the greased frying basket and Air Fry for 10 minutes, flipping them once until the edges are golden. Meanwhile, mix mayonnaise, lemon juice and Cajun seasoning in a small bowl until well blended. Set aside. When you are ready to serve, start with the bottom of the bun. Add a lettuce leaf, then a crab cake. Top with a heaping tbsp of Cajun mayo, minced pickles, and top with the bun and enjoy.

British Fish & Chips

Servings: 4

Cooking Time: 40 Minutes

Ingredients:

- 2 peeled russet potatoes, thinly sliced
- 1 egg white
- 1 tbsp lemon juice
- 1/3 cup ground almonds
- 2 bread slices, crumbled
- ½ tsp dried basil
- 4 haddock fillets

Directions:

1. Preheat air fryer to 390°F. Lay the potato slices in the frying basket and Air Fry for 11-15 minutes. Turn the fries a couple of times while cooking. While the fries are cooking, whisk the egg white and lemon juice together in a bowl. On a plate, combine the almonds, breadcrumbs, and basil. First, one at a time, dip the fillets into the egg mix and then coat in the almond/breadcrumb mix. Lay the fillets on a wire rack until the fries are done. Preheat the oven to 350°F. After the fries are done, move them to a pan and place in the oven to keep warm. Put the fish in the frying basket and Air Fry for 10-14 minutes or until cooked through, golden, and crispy. Serve with the fries.

Crab Cakes On A Budget

Servings: 4

Cooking Time: 12 Minutes

Ingredients:

- 8 ounces imitation crabmeat
- 4 ounces leftover cooked fish (such as cod, pollock, or haddock)
- 2 tablespoons minced green onion
- 2 tablespoons minced celery
- ¾ cup crushed saltine cracker crumbs
- 2 tablespoons light mayonnaise
- 1 teaspoon prepared yellow mustard
- 1 tablespoon Worcestershire sauce, plus 2 teaspoons
- 2 teaspoons dried parsley flakes
- ½ teaspoon dried dill weed, crushed
- ½ teaspoon garlic powder
- ½ teaspoon Old Bay Seasoning
- ½ cup panko breadcrumbs
- oil for misting or cooking spray

Directions:

1. Use knives or a food processor to finely shred crabmeat and fish.
2. In a large bowl, combine all ingredients except panko and oil. Stir well.
3. Shape into 8 small, fat patties.
4. Carefully roll patties in panko crumbs to coat. Spray both sides with oil or cooking spray.
5. Place patties in air fryer basket and cook at 390°F for 12 minutes or until golden brown and crispy.

Shrimp Patties

Servings: 4
Cooking Time: 10 Minutes
Ingredients:

- ½ pound shelled and deveined raw shrimp
- ¼ cup chopped red bell pepper
- ¼ cup chopped green onion
- ¼ cup chopped celery
- 2 cups cooked sushi rice
- ½ teaspoon garlic powder
- ½ teaspoon Old Bay Seasoning
- ½ teaspoon salt
- 2 teaspoons Worcestershire sauce
- ½ cup plain breadcrumbs
- oil for misting or cooking spray

Directions:

1. Finely chop the shrimp. You can do this in a food processor, but it takes only a few pulses. Be careful not to overprocess into mush.
2. Place shrimp in a large bowl and add all other ingredients except the breadcrumbs and oil. Stir until well combined.
3. Preheat air fryer to 390°F.
4. Shape shrimp mixture into 8 patties, no more than ½-inch thick. Roll patties in breadcrumbs and mist with oil or cooking spray.
5. Place 4 shrimp patties in air fryer basket and cook at 390°F for 10 minutes, until shrimp cooks through and outside is crispy.
6. Repeat step 5 to cook remaining shrimp patties.

Sweet & Spicy Swordfish Kebabs

Servings: 4
Cooking Time: 30 Minutes
Ingredients:

- ½ cup canned pineapple chunks, drained, juice reserved
- 1 lb swordfish steaks, cubed
- ½ cup large red grapes
- 1 tbsp honey
- 2 tsp grated fresh ginger
- 1 tsp olive oil
- Pinch cayenne pepper

Directions:

1. Preheat air fryer to 370°F. Poke 8 bamboo skewers through the swordfish, pineapple, and grapes. Mix the honey, 1 tbsp of pineapple juice, ginger, olive oil, and cayenne in a bowl, then use a brush to rub the mix on the kebabs. Allow the marinate to sit on the kebab for 10 minutes. Grill the kebabs for 8-12 minutes until the fish is cooked through and the fruit is soft and glazed. Brush the kebabs again with the mix, then toss the rest of the marinade. Serve warm and enjoy!

Crab Cakes

Servings: 2
Cooking Time: 10 Minutes
Ingredients:

- 1 teaspoon butter
- ⅓ cup finely diced onion
- ⅓ cup finely diced celery
- ¼ cup mayonnaise
- 1 teaspoon Dijon mustard
- 1 egg
- pinch ground cayenne pepper
- 1 teaspoon salt
- freshly ground black pepper
- 16 ounces lump crabmeat
- ½ cup + 2 tablespoons panko breadcrumbs, divided

Directions:

1. Melt the butter in a skillet over medium heat. Sauté the onion and celery until it starts to soften, but not brown – about 4 minutes. Transfer the cooked vegetables to a large bowl. Add the mayonnaise, Dijon mustard, egg, cayenne pepper, salt and freshly ground black pepper to the bowl. Gently fold in the lump crabmeat and 2 tablespoons of panko breadcrumbs. Stir carefully so you don't break up all the crab pieces.
2. Preheat the air fryer to 400°F.
3. Place the remaining panko breadcrumbs in a shallow dish. Divide the crab mixture into 4 portions and shape each portion into a round patty. Dredge the crab patties in the breadcrumbs, coating both sides as well as the edges with the crumbs.
4. Air-fry the crab cakes for 5 minutes. Using a flat spatula, gently turn the cakes over and air-fry for another 5 minutes. Serve the crab cakes with tartar sauce or cocktail sauce, or dress it up with the suggestion below.

Horseradish Tuna Croquettes

Servings:4
Cooking Time: 40 Minutes
Ingredients:

- 1 can tuna in water, drained
- 1/3 cup mayonnaise
- 1 tbsp minced celery
- 1 green onion, sliced
- 2 tsp dried dill
- 1 tsp lime juice
- 1 cup bread crumbs
- 1 egg
- 1 tsp prepared horseradish

Directions:

1. Preheat air fryer to 370ºF. Add the tuna, mayonnaise, celery, green onion, dill, lime juice, ¼ cup bread crumbs, egg, and horseradish in a bowl and mix to combine. Mold the mixture into 12 rectangular mound shapes. Roll each croquette in a shallow dish with 3/4 cup of bread crumbs. Place croquettes in the lightly greased frying basket and Air Fry for 12 minutes on all sides. Serve.

Coconut Jerk Shrimp

Servings:3
Cooking Time: 8 Minutes
Ingredients:

- 1 Large egg white(s)
- 1 teaspoon Purchased or homemade jerk dried seasoning blend (see the headnote)
- ¾ cup Plain panko bread crumbs (gluten-free, if a concern)
- ¾ cup Unsweetened shredded coconut
- 12 Large shrimp (20–25 per pound), peeled and deveined
- Coconut oil spray

Directions:

1. Preheat the air fryer to 375°F .
2. Whisk the egg white(s) and seasoning blend in a bowl until foamy. Add the shrimp and toss well to coat evenly.
3. Mix the bread crumbs and coconut on a dinner plate until well combined. Use kitchen tongs to pick up a shrimp, letting the excess egg white mixture slip back into the rest. Set the shrimp in the bread-crumb mixture. Turn several times to coat evenly and thoroughly. Set on a cutting board and continue coating the remainder of the shrimp.
4. Lightly coat all the shrimp on both sides with the coconut oil spray. Set them in the basket in one layer with as much space between them as possible. (You can even stand some up along the basket's wall in some models.) Air-fry undisturbed for 6 minutes, or until the coating is lightly browned. If the air fryer is at 360°F, you may need to add 2 minutes to the cooking time.
5. Use clean kitchen tongs to transfer the shrimp to a wire rack. Cool for only a minute or two before serving.

Spiced Shrimp Empanadas

Servings: 5
Cooking Time: 30 Minutes
Ingredients:

- ½ lb peeled and deveined shrimp, chopped
- 2 tbsp diced red bell peppers
- 1 shallot, minced
- 1 scallion, chopped
- 2 garlic cloves, minced
- 2 tbsp chopped cilantro
- ½ tbsp lemon juice
- ¼ tsp sweet paprika
- ⅛ tsp salt
- ⅛ tsp red pepper flakes
- ¼ tsp ground nutmeg
- 1 large egg, beaten
- 10 empanada discs

Directions:

1. Combine all ingredients, except the egg and empanada discs, in a bowl. Toss to coat. Beat the 1 egg with 1 tsp of water in a small bowl until blended. Set aside.
2. On your work board, place one empanada disc. Add 2 tbsp of shrimp mixture in the middle. Brush the edges of the disc with the egg mixture. Fold the disc in half and seal the edges. Crimp with a fork by pressing around the edges. Brush the tops with the egg mixture. Preheat air fryer to 380°F. Put the empanadas in the greased frying basket and Air Fry for 9 minutes, flipping once until golden and crispy. Serve hot.

Smoked Paprika Cod Goujons

Servings: 2
Cooking Time: 30 Minutes
Ingredients:

- 1 cod fillet, cut into chunks
- 2 eggs, beaten
- ¼ cup breadcrumbs
- ¼ cup rice flour
- 1 lemon, juiced
- ½ tbsp garlic powder
- 1 tsp smoked paprika
- Salt and pepper to taste

Directions:

1. Preheat air fryer to 350°F. In a bowl, stir the beaten eggs and lemon juice thoroughly. Dip the cod chunks in the mixture. In another bowl, mix the bread crumbs, rice flour, garlic powder, smoked paprika, salt, and pepper.
2. Coat the cod with the crumb mixture. Transfer the coated cod to the greased frying basket. Air Fry for 14-16 minutes until the fish goujons are cooked through and their crust is golden, brown, and delicious. Toss the basket two or three times during the cooking time. Serve.

Mom´s Tuna Melt Toastie

Servings: 4
Cooking Time: 30 Minutes
Ingredients:

- 4 white bread slices
- 2 oz canned tuna
- 2 tbsp mayonnaise
- ½ lemon, zested and juiced
- Salt and pepper to taste
- ½ red onion, finely sliced
- 1 red tomato, sliced
- 4 cheddar cheese slices
- 2 tbsp butter, melted

Directions:

1. Preheat air fryer to 360°F. Put the butter-greased bread slices in the frying basket. Toast for 6 minutes. Meanwhile, mix the tuna, lemon juice and zest, salt, pepper, and mayonnaise in a small bowl. When the time is over, slide the frying basket out, flip the bread slices, and spread the tuna mixture evenly all over them. Cover with tomato slices, red onion, and cheddar cheese. Toast for 10 minutes or until the cheese is melted and lightly bubbling. Serve and enjoy!

Stuffed Shrimp

Servings: 4
Cooking Time: 12 Minutes Per Batch
Ingredients:

- 16 tail-on shrimp, peeled and deveined (last tail section intact)
- ¾ cup crushed panko breadcrumbs
- oil for misting or cooking spray
- Stuffing
- 2 6-ounce cans lump crabmeat
- 2 tablespoons chopped shallots
- 2 tablespoons chopped green onions
- 2 tablespoons chopped celery
- 2 tablespoons chopped green bell pepper
- ½ cup crushed saltine crackers
- 1 teaspoon Old Bay Seasoning
- 1 teaspoon garlic powder
- ¼ teaspoon ground thyme
- 2 teaspoons dried parsley flakes
- 2 teaspoons fresh lemon juice
- 2 teaspoons Worcestershire sauce
- 1 egg, beaten

Directions:

1. Rinse shrimp. Remove tail section (shell) from 4 shrimp, discard, and chop the meat finely.
2. To prepare the remaining 12 shrimp, cut a deep slit down the back side so that the meat lies open flat. Do not cut all the way through.
3. Preheat air fryer to 360°F.
4. Place chopped shrimp in a large bowl with all of the stuffing ingredients and stir to combine.
5. Divide stuffing into 12 portions, about 2 tablespoons each.
6. Place one stuffing portion onto the back of each shrimp and form into a ball or oblong shape. Press firmly so that stuffing sticks together and adheres to shrimp.
7. Gently roll each stuffed shrimp in panko crumbs and mist with oil or cooking spray.
8. Place 6 shrimp in air fryer basket and cook at 360°F for 10minutes. Mist with oil or spray and cook 2 minutes longer or until stuffing cooks through inside and is crispy outside.
9. Repeat step 8 to cook remaining shrimp.

Potato Chip-crusted Cod

Servings: 2
Cooking Time: 20 Minutes

Ingredients:

- ½ cup crushed potato chips
- 1 tsp chopped tarragon
- 1/8 tsp salt
- 1 tsp cayenne powder
- 1 tbsp Dijon mustard
- ¼ cup buttermilk
- 1 tsp lemon juice
- 1 tbsp butter, melted
- 2 cod fillets

Directions:

1. Preheat air fryer at 350°F. Mix all ingredients in a bowl. Press potato chip mixture evenly across tops of cod. Place cod fillets in the greased frying basket and Air Fry for 10 minutes until the fish is opaque and flakes easily with a fork. Serve immediately.

Cajun Flounder Fillets

Servings:2
Cooking Time: 5 Minutes

Ingredients:

- 2 4-ounce skinless flounder fillet(s)
- 2 teaspoons Peanut oil
- 1 teaspoon Purchased or homemade Cajun dried seasoning blend (see the headnote)

Directions:

1. Preheat the air fryer to 400°F.
2. Oil the fillet(s) by drizzling on the peanut oil, then gently rubbing in the oil with your clean, dry fingers. Sprinkle the seasoning blend evenly over both sides of the fillet(s).
3. When the machine is at temperature, set the fillet(s) in the basket. If working with more than one fillet, they should not touch, although they may be quite close together, depending on the basket's size. Air-fry undisturbed for 5 minutes, or until lightly browned and cooked through.
4. Use a nonstick-safe spatula to transfer the fillets to a serving platter or plate(s). Serve at once.

Sriracha Salmon Melt Sandwiches

Servings: 4
Cooking Time: 20 Minutes

Ingredients:

- 2 tbsp butter, softened
- 2 cans pink salmon
- 2 English muffins
- 1/3 cup mayonnaise
- 2 tbsp Dijon mustard
- 1 tbsp fresh lemon juice
- 1/3 cup chopped celery
- ½ tsp sriracha sauce
- 4 slices tomato
- 4 slices Swiss cheese

Directions:

1. Preheat the air fryer to 370°F. Split the English muffins with a fork and spread butter on the 4 halves. Put the halves in the basket and Bake for 3-5 minutes, or until toasted. Remove and set aside. Combine the salmon, mayonnaise, mustard, lemon juice, celery, and sriracha in a bowl. Divide among the English muffin halves. Top each sandwich with tomato and cheese and put in the frying basket. Bake for 4-6 minutes or until the cheese is melted and starts to brown. Serve hot.

Tuscan Salmon

Servings: 4
Cooking Time: 15 Minutes

Ingredients:

- 2 tbsp olive oil
- 4 salmon fillets
- ½ tsp salt
- ¼ tsp red pepper flakes
- 1 tsp chopped dill
- 2 tomatoes, diced
- ¼ cup sliced black olives
- 4 lemon slices

Directions:

1. Preheat air fryer to 380°F. Lightly brush the olive oil on both sides of the salmon fillets and season them with salt, red flakes, and dill. Put the fillets in a single layer in the frying basket, then layer the tomatoes and black olives over the top. Top each fillet with a lemon slice. Bake for 8 minutes. Serve and enjoy!

Tilapia Teriyaki

Servings: 3
Cooking Time: 10 Minutes

Ingredients:

- 4 tablespoons teriyaki sauce
- 1 tablespoon pineapple juice
- 1 pound tilapia fillets
- cooking spray
- 6 ounces frozen mixed peppers with onions, thawed and drained
- 2 cups cooked rice

Directions:

1. Mix the teriyaki sauce and pineapple juice together in a small bowl.
2. Split tilapia fillets down the center lengthwise.
3. Brush all sides of fish with the sauce, spray air fryer basket with nonstick cooking spray, and place fish in the basket.
4. Stir the peppers and onions into the remaining sauce and spoon over the fish. Save any leftover sauce for drizzling over the fish when serving.
5. Cook at 360°F for 10 minutes, until fish flakes easily with a fork and is done in center.
6. Divide into 3 or 4 servings and serve each with approximately ½ cup cooked rice.

Nutty Shrimp With Amaretto Glaze

Servings: 10
Cooking Time: 10 Minutes

Ingredients:

- 1 cup flour
- ½ teaspoon baking powder
- 1 teaspoon salt
- 2 eggs, beaten
- ½ cup milk
- 2 tablespoons olive or vegetable oil
- 2 cups sliced almonds
- 2 pounds large shrimp (about 32 to 40 shrimp), peeled and deveined, tails left on
- 2 cups amaretto liqueur

Directions:

1. Combine the flour, baking powder and salt in a large bowl. Add the eggs, milk and oil and stir until it forms a smooth batter. Coarsely crush the sliced almonds into a second shallow dish with your hands.
2. Dry the shrimp well with paper towels. Dip the shrimp into the batter and shake off any excess batter, leaving just enough to lightly coat the shrimp. Transfer the shrimp to the dish with the almonds and coat completely. Place the coated shrimp on a plate or baking sheet and when all the shrimp have been coated, freeze the shrimp for an 1 hour, or as long as a week before air-frying.
3. Preheat the air fryer to 400°F.
4. Transfer 8 frozen shrimp at a time to the air fryer basket. Air-fry for 6 minutes. Turn the shrimp over and air-fry for an additional 4 minutes. Repeat with the remaining shrimp.
5. While the shrimp are cooking, bring the Amaretto to a boil in a small saucepan on the stovetop. Lower the heat and simmer until it has reduced and thickened into a glaze – about 10 minutes.
6. Remove the shrimp from the air fryer and brush both sides with the warm amaretto glaze. Serve warm.

Mojo Sea Bass

Servings:2
Cooking Time: 15 Minutes

Ingredients:

- 1 tbsp butter, melted
- ¼ tsp chili powder
- 2 cloves garlic, minced
- 1 tbsp lemon juice
- ¼ tsp salt
- 2 sea bass fillets
- 2 tsp chopped cilantro

Directions:

1. Preheat air fryer to 370°F. Whisk the butter, chili powder, garlic, lemon juice, and salt in a bowl. Rub mixture over the tops of each fillet. Place the fillets in the frying basket and Air Fry for 7 minutes. Let rest for 5 minutes. Divide between 2 plates and garnish with cilantro to serve.

Lemon-roasted Salmon Fillets

Servings:3

Cooking Time: 7 Minutes

Ingredients:

- 3 6-ounce skin-on salmon fillets
- Olive oil spray
- 9 Very thin lemon slices
- ¾ teaspoon Ground black pepper
- ¼ teaspoon Table salt

Directions:

1. Preheat the air fryer to 400°F.
2. Generously coat the skin of each of the fillets with olive oil spray. Set the fillets skin side down on your work surface. Place three overlapping lemon slices down the length of each salmon fillet. Sprinkle them with the pepper and salt. Coat lightly with olive oil spray.
3. Use a nonstick-safe spatula to transfer the fillets one by one to the basket, leaving as much air space between them as possible. Air-fry undisturbed for 7 minutes, or until cooked through.
4. Use a nonstick-safe spatula to transfer the fillets to serving plates. Cool for only a minute or two before serving.

Easy-peasy Shrimp

Servings:2

Cooking Time: 15 Minutes

Ingredients:

- 1 lb tail-on shrimp, deveined
- 2 tbsp butter, melted
- 1 tbsp lemon juice
- 1 tbsp dill, chopped

Directions:

1. Preheat air fryer to 350°F. Combine shrimp and butter in a bowl. Place shrimp in the greased frying basket and Air Fry for 6 minutes, flipping once. Squeeze lemon juice over and top with dill. Serve hot.

Better Fish Sticks

Servings:3

Cooking Time: 8 Minutes

Ingredients:

- ¾ cup Seasoned Italian-style dried bread crumbs (gluten-free, if a concern)
- 3 tablespoons (about ½ ounce) Finely grated Parmesan cheese
- 10 ounces Skinless cod fillets, cut lengthwise into 1-inch-wide pieces
- 3 tablespoons Regular or low-fat mayonnaise (not fat-free; gluten-free, if a concern)
- Vegetable oil spray

Directions:

1. Preheat the air fryer to 400°F.
2. Mix the bread crumbs and grated Parmesan in a shallow soup bowl or a small pie plate.
3. Smear the fish fillet sticks completely with the mayonnaise, then dip them one by one in the bread-crumb mixture, turning and pressing gently to make an even and thorough coating. Coat each stick on all sides with vegetable oil spray.
4. Set the fish sticks in the basket with at least ¼ inch between them. Air-fry undisturbed for 8 minutes, or until golden brown and crisp.
5. Use a nonstick-safe spatula to gently transfer them from the basket to a wire rack. Cool for only a minute or two before serving.

Californian Tilapia

Servings: 4

Cooking Time: 15 Minutes

Ingredients:

- Salt and pepper to taste
- ¼ tsp garlic powder
- ¼ tsp chili powder
- ¼ tsp dried oregano
- ¼ tsp smoked paprika
- 1 tbsp butter, melted
- 4 tilapia fillets
- 2 tbsp lime juice
- 1 lemon, sliced

Directions:

1. Preheat air fryer to 400°F. Combine salt, pepper, oregano, garlic powder, chili powder, and paprika in a small bowl. Place tilapia in a pie pan, then pour lime juice and butter over the fish. Season both sides of the fish with the spice blend. Arrange the tilapia in a single layer of the parchment-lined frying basket without touching each other. Air Fry for 4 minutes, then carefully flip the fish. Air Fry for another 4 to 5 minutes until the fish is cooked and the outside is crispy. Serve immediately with lemon slices on the side and enjoy.

Lime Halibut Parcels

Servings: 4
Cooking Time: 45 Minutes
Ingredients:

- 1 lime, sliced
- 4 halibut fillets
- 1 tsp dried thyme
- Salt and pepper to taste
- 1 shredded carrot
- 1 red bell pepper, sliced
- ½ cup sliced celery
- 2 tbsp butter

Directions:

1. Preheat the air fryer to 400°F. Tear off four 14-inch lengths of parchment paper and fold each piece in half crosswise. Put the lime slices in the center of half of each piece of paper, then top with halibut. Sprinkle each filet with thyme, salt, and pepper, then top each with ¼ of the carrots, bell pepper, and celery. Add a dab of butter. Fold the parchment paper in half and crimp the edges all around to enclose the halibut and vegetables. Put one parchment bundle in the basket, add a raised rack, and add another bundle. Bake for 12-14 minutes or until the bundle puff up. The fish should flake with a fork; put the bundles in the oven to keep warm. Repeat for the second batch of parchment bundles. Hot steam will be released when the bundles are opened.

Black Cod With Grapes, Fennel, Pecans And Kale

Servings: 2
Cooking Time: 15 Minutes
Ingredients:

- 2 (6- to 8-ounce) fillets of black cod (or sablefish)
- salt and freshly ground black pepper
- olive oil
- 1 cup grapes, halved
- 1 small bulb fennel, sliced ¼-inch thick
- ½ cup pecans
- 3 cups shredded kale
- 2 teaspoons white balsamic vinegar or white wine vinegar
- 2 tablespoons extra virgin olive oil

Directions:

1. Preheat the air fryer to 400°F.
2. Season the cod fillets with salt and pepper and drizzle, brush or spray a little olive oil on top. Place the fish, presentation side up (skin side down), into the air fryer basket. Air-fry for 10 minutes.
3. When the fish has finished cooking, remove the fillets to a side plate and loosely tent with foil to rest.
4. Toss the grapes, fennel and pecans in a bowl with a drizzle of olive oil and season with salt and pepper. Add the grapes, fennel and pecans to the air fryer basket and air-fry for 5 minutes at 400°F, shaking the basket once during the cooking time.
5. Transfer the grapes, fennel and pecans to a bowl with the kale. Dress the kale with the balsamic vinegar and olive oil, season to taste with salt and pepper and serve along side the cooked fish.

Sardinas Fritas

Servings: 2
Cooking Time: 15 Minutes
Ingredients:

- 2 cans boneless, skinless sardines in mustard sauce
- Salt and pepper to taste
- ½ cup bread crumbs
- 2 lemon wedges
- 1 tsp chopped parsley

Directions:

1. Preheat air fryer at 350°F. Add breadcrumbs, salt and black pepper to a bowl. Roll sardines in the breadcrumbs to coat. Place them in the greased frying basket and Air Fry for 6 minutes, flipping once. Transfer them to a serving dish. Serve topped with parsley and lemon wedges.

Sea Bass With Fruit Salsa

Servings: 4
Cooking Time: 30 Minutes
Ingredients:

- 3 halved nectarines, pitted
- 4 sea bass fillets
- 2 tsp olive oil
- 3 plums, halved and pitted
- 1 cup red grapes
- 1 tbsp lemon juice
- 1 tbsp honey
- ½ tsp dried thyme

Directions:

1. Preheat air fryer to 390°F. Lay the sea bass fillets in the frying basket, then spritz olive oil over the top. Air Fry for 4 minutes. Take the basket out of the fryer and add the nectarines and plums. Pour the grapes over, spritz with lemon juice and honey, then add a pinch of thyme. Put the basket back into the fryer and Bake for 5-9 minutes. The fish should flake when finished, and the fruits should be soft. Serve hot.

Fish Piccata With Crispy Potatoes

Servings: 4
Cooking Time: 30 Minutes
Ingredients:

- 4 cod fillets
- 1 tbsp butter
- 2 tsp capers
- 1 garlic clove, minced
- 2 tbsp lemon juice
- ½ lb asparagus, trimmed
- 2 large potatoes, cubed
- 1 tbsp olive oil
- Salt and pepper to taste
- ¼ tsp garlic powder
- 1 tsp dried rosemary
- 1 tsp dried parsley
- 1 tsp chopped dill

Directions:

1. Preheat air fryer to 380°F. Place each fillet on a large piece of foil. Top each fillet with butter, capers, dill, garlic, and lemon juice. Fold the foil over the fish and seal the edges to make a pouch. Mix asparagus, parsley, potatoes, olive oil, salt, rosemary, garlic powder, and pepper in a large bowl. Place asparagus in the frying basket. Roast for 4 minutes, then shake the basket. Top vegetable with foil packets and Roast for another 8 minutes. Turn off air fryer and let it stand for 5 minutes. Serve warm and enjoy.

Mediterranean Salmon Cakes

Servings:4
Cooking Time: 30 Minutes
Ingredients:

- ¼ cup heavy cream
- 5 tbsp mayonnaise
- 2 cloves garlic, minced
- ¼ tsp caper juice
- 2 tsp lemon juice
- 1 tbsp capers
- 1 can salmon
- 2 tsp lemon zest
- 1 egg
- ¼ minced red bell peppers
- ½ cup flour
- ⅛ tsp salt
- 2 tbsp sliced green olives

Directions:

1. Combine heavy cream, 2 tbsp of mayonnaise, garlic, caper juices, capers, and lemon juice in a bowl. Place the resulting caper sauce in the fridge until ready to use.
2. Preheat air fryer to 400°F. Combine canned salmon, lemon zest, egg, remaining mayo, bell peppers, flour, and salt in a bowl. Form into 8 patties. Place the patties in the greased frying basket and Air Fry for 10 minutes, turning once. Let rest for 5 minutes before drizzling with lemon sauce. Garnish with green olives to serve.

Halibut Quesadillas

Servings: 2
Cooking Time: 30 Minutes
Ingredients:

- ¼ cup shredded cheddar
- ¼ cup shredded mozzarella
- 1 tsp olive oil
- 2 tortilla shells
- 1 halibut fillet
- ½ peeled avocado, sliced
- 1 garlic clove, minced
- Salt and pepper to taste
- ½ tsp lemon juice

Directions:

1. Preheat air fryer to 350°F. Brush the halibut fillet with olive oil and sprinkle with salt and pepper. Bake in the air fryer for 12-14 minutes, flipping once until cooked through. Combine the avocado, garlic, salt, pepper, and lemon juice in a bowl and, using a fork, mash lightly until the avocado is slightly chunky. Add and spread the resulting guacamole on one tortilla. Top with the cooked fish and cheeses, and cover with the second tortilla. Bake in the air fryer 6-8, flipping once until the cheese is melted. Serve immediately.

Crispy Smelts

Servings:3

Cooking Time: 20 Minutes

Ingredients:

- 1 pound Cleaned smelts
- 3 tablespoons Tapioca flour
- Vegetable oil spray
- To taste Coarse sea salt or kosher salt

Directions:

1. Preheat the air fryer to 400°F.
2. Toss the smelts and tapioca flour in a large bowl until the little fish are evenly coated.
3. Lay the smelts out on a large cutting board. Lightly coat both sides of each fish with vegetable oil spray.
4. When the machine is at temperature, set the smelts close together in the basket, with a few even overlapping on top. Air-fry undisturbed for 20 minutes, until lightly browned and crisp.
5. Remove the basket from the machine and turn out the fish onto a wire rack. The smelts will most likely come out as one large block, or maybe in a couple of large pieces. Cool for a minute or two, then sprinkle the smelts with salt and break the block(s) into much smaller sections or individual fish to serve.

Horseradish Crusted Salmon

Servings: 2

Cooking Time: 14 Minutes

Ingredients:

- 2 (5-ounce) salmon fillets
- salt and freshly ground black pepper
- 2 teaspoons Dijon mustard
- ½ cup panko breadcrumbs*
- 2 tablespoons prepared horseradish
- ½ teaspoon finely chopped lemon zest
- 1 tablespoon olive oil
- 1 tablespoon chopped fresh parsley

Directions:

1. Preheat the air fryer to 360°F.
2. Season the salmon with salt and freshly ground black pepper. Then spread the Dijon mustard on the salmon, coating the entire surface.
3. Combine the breadcrumbs, horseradish, lemon zest and olive oil in a small bowl. Spread the mixture over the top of the salmon and press down lightly with your hands, adhering it to the salmon using the mustard as "glue".
4. Transfer the salmon to the air fryer basket and air-fry at 360°F for 14 minutes (depending on how thick your fillet is) or until the fish feels firm to the touch. Sprinkle with the parsley.

Herb-crusted Sole

Servings: 4

Cooking Time: 20 Minutes

Ingredients:

- ½ lemon, juiced and zested
- 4 sole fillets
- ½ tsp dried thyme
- ½ tsp dried marjoram
- ½ tsp dried parsley
- Black pepper to taste
- 1 bread slice, crumbled
- 2 tsp olive oil

Directions:

1. Preheat air fryer to 320°F. In a bowl, combine the lemon zest, thyme, marjoram, parsley, pepper, breadcrumbs, and olive oil and stir. Arrange the sole fillets on a lined baking pan, skin-side down. Pour the lemon juice over the fillets, then press them firmly into the breadcrumb mixture to coat. Air Fry for 8-11 minutes, until the breadcrumbs are crisp and golden brown. Serve warm.

Shrimp Teriyaki

Servings:10

Cooking Time: 6 Minutes

Ingredients:

- 1 tablespoon Regular or low-sodium soy sauce or gluten-free tamari sauce
- 1 tablespoon Mirin or a substitute (see here)
- 1 teaspoon Ginger juice (see the headnote)
- 10 Large shrimp (20–25 per pound), peeled and deveined
- ⅔ cup Plain panko bread crumbs (gluten-free, if a concern)
- 1 Large egg
- Vegetable oil spray

Directions:

1. Whisk the soy or tamari sauce, mirin, and ginger juice in an 8- or 9-inch square baking pan until uniform. Add the shrimp and toss well to coat. Cover and refrigerate for 1 hour, tossing the shrimp in the marinade at least twice.
2. Preheat the air fryer to 400°F.
3. Thread a marinated shrimp on a 4-inch bamboo skewer by inserting the pointy tip at the small end of the shrimp, then guiding the skewer along the shrimp so that the tip comes out the thick end and the shrimp

is flat along the length of the skewer. Repeat with the remaining shrimp. (You'll need eight 4-inch skewers for the small batch, 10 skewers for the medium batch, and 12 for the large.)

4. Pour the bread crumbs onto a dinner plate. Whisk the egg in the baking pan with any marinade that stayed behind. Lay the skewers in the pan, in as close to a single layer as possible. Turn repeatedly to make sure the shrimp is coated in the egg mixture.
5. One at a time, take a skewered shrimp out of the pan and set it in the bread crumbs, turning several times and pressing gently until the shrimp is evenly coated on all sides. Coat the shrimp with vegetable oil spray and set the skewer aside. Repeat with the remainder of the shrimp.
6. Set the skewered shrimp in the basket in one layer. Air-fry undisturbed for 6 minutes, or until pink and firm.
7. Transfer the skewers to a wire rack. Cool for only a minute or two before serving.

Sea Scallops

Servings: 4
Cooking Time: 8 Minutes

Ingredients:

- 1½ pounds sea scallops
- salt and pepper
- 2 eggs
- ½ cup flour
- ½ cup plain breadcrumbs
- oil for misting or cooking spray

Directions:

1. Rinse scallops and remove the tough side muscle. Sprinkle to taste with salt and pepper.
2. Beat eggs together in a shallow dish. Place flour in a second shallow dish and breadcrumbs in a third.
3. Preheat air fryer to 390°F.
4. Dip scallops in flour, then eggs, and then roll in breadcrumbs. Mist with oil or cooking spray.
5. Place scallops in air fryer basket in a single layer, leaving some space between. You should be able to cook about a dozen at a time.
6. Cook at 390°F for 8 minutes, watching carefully so as not to overcook. Scallops are done when they turn opaque all the way through. They will feel slightly firm when pressed with tines of a fork.
7. Repeat step 6 to cook remaining scallops.

Garlic-butter Lobster Tails

Servings:2
Cooking Time: 20 Minutes

Ingredients:

- 2 lobster tails
- 1 tbsp butter, melted
- ½ tsp Old Bay Seasoning
- ½ tsp garlic powder
- 1 tbsp chopped parsley
- 2 lemon wedges

Directions:

1. Preheat air fryer to 400°F. Using kitchen shears, cut down the middle of each lobster tail on the softer side. Carefully run your finger between the lobster meat and the shell to loosen the meat. Place lobster tails in the frying basket, cut sides up, and Air Fry for 4 minutes. Rub with butter, garlic powder and Old Bay seasoning and cook for 4 more minutes. Garnish with parsley and lemon wedges. Serve and enjoy!

Sweet Potato–wrapped Shrimp

Servings:3
Cooking Time: 6 Minutes

Ingredients:

- 24 Long spiralized sweet potato strands
- Olive oil spray
- ¼ teaspoon Garlic powder
- ¼ teaspoon Table salt
- Up to a ⅛ teaspoon Cayenne
- 12 Large shrimp (20–25 per pound), peeled and deveined

Directions:

1. Preheat the air fryer to 400°F.
2. Lay the spiralized sweet potato strands on a large swath of paper towels and straighten out the strands to long ropes. Coat them with olive oil spray, then sprinkle them with the garlic powder, salt, and cayenne.
3. Pick up 2 strands and wrap them around the center of a shrimp, with the ends tucked under what now becomes the bottom side of the shrimp. Continue wrapping the remainder of the shrimp.
4. Set the shrimp bottom side down in the basket with as much air space between them as possible. Air-fry undisturbed for 6 minutes, or until the sweet potato strands are crisp and the shrimp are pink and firm.
5. Use kitchen tongs to transfer the shrimp to a wire rack. Cool for only a minute or two before serving.

Creole Tilapia With Garlic Mayo

Servings: 4

Cooking Time: 20 Minutes

Ingredients:

- 4 tilapia fillets
- 2 tbsp olive oil
- 1 tsp paprika
- 1 tsp garlic powder
- 1 tsp dried basil
- ½ tsp Creole seasoning
- ½ tsp chili powder
- 2 garlic cloves, minced
- 1 tbsp mayonnaise
- 1 tsp olive oil
- ½ lemon, juiced
- Salt and pepper to taste

Directions:

1. Preheat air fryer to 400°F. Coat the tilapia with some olive oil, then season with paprika, garlic powder, basil, and Creole seasoning. Bake in the greased frying basket for 15 minutes, flipping once during cooking.
2. While the fish is cooking, whisk together garlic, mayonnaise, olive oil, lemon juice, chili powder, salt and pepper in a bowl. Serve the cooked fish with the aioli.

Desserts And Sweets Recipes

Donut Holes

Servings: 13

Cooking Time: 12 Minutes

Ingredients:

- 6 tablespoons Granulated white sugar
- 1½ tablespoons Butter, melted and cooled
- 2 tablespoons (or 1 small egg, well beaten) Pasteurized egg substitute, such as Egg Beaters
- 6 tablespoons Regular or low-fat sour cream (not fat-free)
- ¾ teaspoon Vanilla extract
- 1⅔ cups All-purpose flour
- ¾ teaspoon Baking powder
- ¼ teaspoon Table salt
- Vegetable oil spray

Directions:

1. Preheat the air fryer to 350°F .
2. Whisk the sugar and melted butter in a medium bowl until well combined. Whisk in the egg substitute or egg , then the sour cream and vanilla until smooth. Remove the whisk and stir in the flour, baking powder, and salt with a wooden spoon just until a soft dough forms.
3. Use 2 tablespoons of this dough to create a ball between your clean palms. Set it aside and continue making balls: 8 more for the small batch, 12 more for the medium batch, or 17 more for the large one.
4. Coat the balls in the vegetable oil spray, then set them in the basket with as much air space between them as possible. Even a fraction of an inch will be enough, but they should not touch. Air-fry undisturbed for 12 minutes, or until browned and cooked through. A toothpick inserted into the center of a ball should come out clean.
5. Pour the contents of the basket onto a wire rack. Cool for at least 5 minutes before serving.

Chocolate Soufflés

Servings: 2

Cooking Time: 14 Minutes

Ingredients:

- butter and sugar for greasing the ramekins
- 3 ounces semi-sweet chocolate, chopped
- ¼ cup unsalted butter
- 2 eggs, yolks and white separated
- 3 tablespoons sugar
- ½ teaspoon pure vanilla extract
- 2 tablespoons all-purpose flour
- powdered sugar, for dusting the finished soufflés
- heavy cream, for serving

Directions:

1. Butter and sugar two 6-ounce ramekins. (Butter the ramekins and then coat the butter with sugar by shaking it around in the ramekin and dumping out any excess.)
2. Melt the chocolate and butter together, either in the microwave or in a double boiler. In a separate bowl, beat the egg yolks vigorously. Add the sugar and the vanilla extract and beat well again. Drizzle in the chocolate and butter, mixing well. Stir in the flour, combining until there are no lumps.
3. Preheat the air fryer to 330°F.
4. In a separate bowl, whisk the egg whites to soft peak stage (the point at which the whites can almost stand up on the end of your whisk). Fold the whipped egg whites into the chocolate mixture gently and in stages.
5. Transfer the batter carefully to the buttered ramekins, leaving about ½-inch at the top. (You may have a little extra batter, depending on how airy the batter is, so you might be able to squeeze out a third soufflé if you want to.) Place the ramekins into the air fryer basket and air-fry for 14 minutes. The soufflés should have risen nicely and be brown on top. (Don't worry if the top gets a little dark – you'll be covering it with powdered sugar in the next step.)
6. Dust with powdered sugar and serve immediately with heavy cream to pour over the top at the table.

Coconut-carrot Cupcakes

Servings: 4
Cooking Time: 25 Minutes
Ingredients:

- 1 cup flour
- ½ tsp baking soda
- 1/3 cup light brown sugar
- ¼ tsp salt
- ¼ tsp ground cinnamon
- 1 ½ tsp vanilla extract
- 1 egg
- 1 tbsp buttermilk
- 1 tbsp vegetable oil
- ¼ cup grated carrots
- 2 tbsp coconut shreds
- 6 oz cream cheese
- 1 1/3 cups powdered sugar
- 2 tbsp butter, softened
- 1 tbsp milk
- 1 tbsp coconut flakes

Directions:

1. Preheat air fryer at 375°F. Combine flour, baking soda, brown sugar, salt, and cinnamon in a bowl. In another bowl, combine egg, 1 tsp of vanilla, buttermilk, and vegetable oil. Pour wet ingredients into dry ingredients and toss to combine. Do not overmix. Fold in carrots and coconut shreds. Spoon mixture into 8 greased silicone cupcake liners. Place cupcakes in the frying basket and Bake for 6-8 minutes. Let cool onto a cooling rack for 15 minutes. Whisk cream cheese, powdered sugar, remaining vanilla, softened butter, and milk in a bowl until smooth. Spread over cooled cupcakes. Garnish with coconut flakes and serve.

Fruity Oatmeal Crisp

Servings: 6
Cooking Time: 25 Minutes
Ingredients:

- 2 peeled nectarines, chopped
- 1 peeled apple, chopped
- 1/3 cup raisins
- 2 tbsp honey
- 1/3 cup brown sugar
- ¼ cup flour
- ½ cup oatmeal
- 3 tbsp softened butter

Directions:

1. Preheat air fryer to 380°F. Mix together nectarines, apple, raisins, and honey in a baking pan. Set aside. Mix brown sugar, flour, oatmeal and butter in a medium bowl until crumbly. Top the fruit in a greased pan with the crumble.Bake until bubbly and the topping is golden, 10-12 minutes. Serve warm and top with vanilla ice cream if desired.

Oreo-coated Peanut Butter Cups

Servings:8
Cooking Time: 4 Minutes
Ingredients:

- 8 Standard ¾-ounce peanut butter cups, frozen
- ⅓ cup All-purpose flour
- 2 Large egg white(s), beaten until foamy
- 16 Oreos or other creme-filled chocolate sandwich cookies, ground to crumbs in a food processor
- Vegetable oil spray

Directions:

1. Set up and fill three shallow soup plates or small pie plates on your counter: one for the flour, one for the beaten egg white(s), and one for the cookie crumbs.

2. Dip a frozen peanut butter cup in the flour, turning it to coat all sides. Shake off any excess, then set it in the beaten egg white(s). Turn it to coat all sides, then let any excess egg white slip back into the rest. Set the candy bar in the cookie crumbs. Turn to coat on all parts, even the sides. Dip the peanut butter cup back in the egg white(s) as before, then into the cookie crumbs as before, making sure you have a solid, even coating all around the cup. Set aside while you dip and coat the remaining cups.
3. When all the peanut butter cups are dipped and coated, lightly coat them on all sides with the vegetable oil spray. Set them on a plate and freeze while the air fryer heats.
4. Preheat the air fryer to 400°F.
5. Set the dipped cups wider side up in the basket with as much air space between them as possible. Air-fry undisturbed for 4 minutes, or until they feel soft but the coating is set.
6. Turn off the machine and remove the basket from it. Set aside the basket with the fried cups for 10 minutes. Use a nonstick-safe spatula to transfer the fried cups to a wire rack. Cool for at least another 5 minutes before serving.

Strawberry Pastry Rolls

Servings: 4
Cooking Time: 6 Minutes
Ingredients:

- 3 ounces low-fat cream cheese
- 2 tablespoons plain yogurt
- 2 teaspoons sugar
- ¼ teaspoon pure vanilla extract
- 8 ounces fresh strawberries
- 8 sheets phyllo dough
- butter-flavored cooking spray
- ¼–½ cup dark chocolate chips (optional)

Directions:

1. In a medium bowl, combine the cream cheese, yogurt, sugar, and vanilla. Beat with hand mixer at high speed until smooth, about 1 minute.
2. Wash strawberries and destem. Chop enough of them to measure ½ cup. Stir into cheese mixture.
3. Preheat air fryer to 330°F.
4. Phyllo dough dries out quickly, so cover your stack of phyllo sheets with waxed paper and then place a damp dish towel on top of that. Remove only one sheet at a time as you work.
5. To create one pastry roll, lay out a single sheet of phyllo. Spray lightly with butter-flavored spray, top with a second sheet of phyllo, and spray the second sheet lightly.
6. Place a quarter of the filling (about 3 tablespoons) about ½ inch from the edge of one short side. Fold the end of the phyllo over the filling and keep rolling a turn or two. Fold in both the left and right sides so that the edges meet in the middle of your roll. Then roll up completely. Spray outside of pastry roll with butter spray.
7. When you have 4 rolls, place them in the air fryer basket, seam side down, leaving some space in between each. Cook at 330°F for 6 minutes, until they turn a delicate golden brown.
8. Repeat step 7 for remaining rolls.
9. Allow pastries to cool to room temperature.
10. When ready to serve, slice the remaining strawberries. If desired, melt the chocolate chips in microwave or double boiler. Place 1 pastry on each dessert plate, and top with sliced strawberries. Drizzle melted chocolate over strawberries and onto plate.

Peach Cobbler

Servings: 4
Cooking Time: 12 Minutes
Ingredients:

- 16 ounces frozen peaches, thawed, with juice (do not drain)
- 6 tablespoons sugar
- 1 tablespoon cornstarch
- 1 tablespoon water
- Crust
- ½ cup flour
- ¼ teaspoon salt
- 3 tablespoons butter
- 1½ tablespoons cold water
- ¼ teaspoon sugar

Directions:

1. Place peaches, including juice, and sugar in air fryer baking pan. Stir to mix well.
2. In a small cup, dissolve cornstarch in the water. Stir into peaches.
3. In a medium bowl, combine the flour and salt. Cut in butter using knives or a pastry blender. Stir in the cold water to make a stiff dough.
4. On a floured board or wax paper, pat dough into a square or circle slightly smaller than your air fryer baking pan. Cut diagonally into 4 pieces.
5. Place dough pieces on top of peaches, leaving a tiny bit of space between the edges. Sprinkle very lightly with sugar, no more than about ¼ teaspoon.

6. Cook at 360°F for 12 minutes, until fruit bubbles and crust browns.

Chocolate Macaroons

Servings: 16
Cooking Time: 8 Minutes

Ingredients:

- 2 Large egg white(s), at room temperature
- 1/8 teaspoon Table salt
- 1/2 cup Granulated white sugar
- 1 1/2 cups Unsweetened shredded coconut
- 3 tablespoons Unsweetened cocoa powder

Directions:

1. Preheat the air fryer to 375°F .
2. Using an electric mixer at high speed, beat the egg white(s) and salt in a medium or large bowl until stiff peaks can be formed when the turned-off beaters are dipped into the mixture.
3. Still working with the mixer at high speed, beat in the sugar in a slow stream until the meringue is shiny and thick.
4. Scrape down and remove the beaters. Fold in the coconut and cocoa with a rubber spatula until well combined, working carefully to deflate the meringue as little as possible.
5. Scoop up 2 tablespoons of the mixture. Wet your clean hands and roll that little bit of coconut bliss into a ball. Set it aside and continue making more balls: 7 more for a small batch, 15 more for a medium batch, or 23 more for a large one.
6. Line the bottom of the machine's basket or the basket attachment with parchment paper. Set the balls on the parchment with as much air space between them as possible. Air-fry undisturbed for 8 minutes, or until dry, set, and lightly browned.
7. Use a nonstick-safe spatula to transfer the macaroons to a wire rack. Cool for at least 10 minutes before serving. Or cool to room temperature, about 30 minutes, then store in a sealed container at room temperature for up to 3 days.

Cinnamon Sugar Banana Rolls

Servings: 6
Cooking Time: 8 Minutes

Ingredients:

- 1/4 cup Granulated white sugar
- 2 teaspoons Ground cinnamon
- 2 tablespoons Peach or apricot jam or orange marmalade
- 6 Spring roll wrappers, thawed if necessary
- 2 Ripe banana(s), peeled and cut into 3-inch-long sections
- 1 Large egg, well beaten
- Vegetable oil spray

Directions:

1. Preheat the air fryer to 400°F.
2. Stir the sugar and cinnamon in a small bowl until well combined. Stir the jam or marmalade with a fork to loosen it up.
3. Set a spring roll wrapper on a clean, dry work surface. Roll a banana section in the sugar mixture until evenly and well coated. Set the coated banana along one edge of the wrapper. Top it with about 1 teaspoon of the jam or marmalade. Fold the sides of the wrapper perpendicular to the banana up and over the banana, partially covering it. Brush beaten egg over the side of the wrapper farthest from the banana. Starting with the banana, roll the wrapper closed, ending at the part with the beaten egg. Press gently to seal. Set the roll aside seam side down and continue filling and rolling the remaining wrappers in the same way.
4. Lightly coat the wrappers with vegetable oil spray. Set them seam side down in the basket with as much air space between them as possible. Air-fry undisturbed for 8 minutes, or until crisp and golden brown.
5. Use kitchen tongs to gently transfer the rolls to a wire rack. Cool for at least 5 minutes or up to 30 minutes before serving.

Baked Stuffed Pears

Servings: 4
Cooking Time: 15 Minutes + Cooling Time

Ingredients:

- 4 cored pears, halved
- 1/2 cup chopped cashews
- 1/2 cup dried cranberries
- 1/4 cup agave nectar
- 1/2 stick butter, softened
- 1/2 tsp ground cinnamon
- 1/2 cup apple juice

Directions:

1. Preheat the air fryer to 350°F. Combine the cashews, cranberries, agave nectar, butter, and cinnamon and mix well. Stuff this mixture into the pears, heaping it up on top. Set the pears in a baking pan and pour the apple juice into the bottom of the pan. Put the pan in the fryer and Bake for 10-12 minutes or until the pears are tender. Let cool before serving.

Lemon Iced Donut Balls

Servings: 6
Cooking Time: 25 Minutes
Ingredients:

- 1 can jumbo biscuit dough
- 2 tsp lemon juice
- ½ cup icing sugar, sifted

Directions:

1. Preheat air fryer to 360°F. Divide the biscuit dough into 16 equal portions. Roll the dough into balls of 1½ inches thickness. Place the donut holes in the greased frying basket and Air Fry for 8 minutes, flipping once. Mix the icing sugar and lemon juice until smooth. Spread the icing over the top of the donuts. Leave to set a bit. Serve.

Keto Cheesecake Cups

Servings: 6
Cooking Time: 10 Minutes
Ingredients:

- 8 ounces cream cheese
- ¼ cup plain whole-milk Greek yogurt
- 1 large egg
- 1 teaspoon pure vanilla extract
- 3 tablespoons monk fruit sweetener
- ¼ teaspoon salt
- ½ cup walnuts, roughly chopped

Directions:

1. Preheat the air fryer to 315°F.
2. In a large bowl, use a hand mixer to beat the cream cheese together with the yogurt, egg, vanilla, sweetener, and salt. When combined, fold in the chopped walnuts.
3. Set 6 silicone muffin liners inside an air-fryer-safe pan. Note: This is to allow for an easier time getting the cheesecake bites in and out. If you don't have a pan, you can place them directly in the air fryer basket.
4. Evenly fill the cupcake liners with cheesecake batter.
5. Carefully place the pan into the air fryer basket and cook for about 10 minutes, or until the tops are lightly browned and firm.
6. Carefully remove the pan when done and place in the refrigerator for 3 hours to firm up before serving.

Greek Pumpkin Cheesecake

Servings: 4
Cooking Time: 35 Minutes + Chilling Time
Ingredients:

- 2 tbsp peanut butter
- ¼ cup oat flour
- ½ cup Greek yogurt
- 2 tbsp sugar
- ¼ cup ricotta cheese
- ¼ cup canned pumpkin
- 1 tbsp vanilla extract
- 2 tbsp cornstarch
- ¼ tsp ground cinnamon

Directions:

1. Preheat air fryer to 320°F. For the crust: Whisk the peanut butter, oat flour, 1 tbsp of Greek yogurt, and 1 tsp of sugar until you get a dough. Remove the dough onto a small cake pan and press down to get a ½-inch thick crust. Set aside. Mix the ricotta cheese, pumpkin, vanilla extract, cornstarch, cinnamon, ½ cup of Greek yogurt, and 1 tbsp of sugar until smooth. Pour over the crust and Bake for 20 minutes until golden brown. Let cool completely and refrigerate for 1 hour before serving.

Banana Fritters

Servings: 6
Cooking Time: 20 Minutes
Ingredients:

- 1 egg
- ¼ cup cornstarch
- ¼ cup bread crumbs
- 3 bananas, halved crosswise
- ¼ cup caramel sauce

Directions:

1. Preheat air fryer to 350°F. Set up three small bowls. In the first bowl, add cornstarch. In the second bowl, beat the egg. In the third bowl, add bread crumbs. Dip the bananas in the cornstarch first, then the egg, and then dredge in bread crumbs. Put the bananas in the greased frying basket and spray with oil. Air Fry for 8 minutes, flipping once around minute 5. Remove to a serving plate and drizzle with caramel sauce. Serve warm and enjoy.

Dark Chocolate Peanut Butter S'mores

Servings: 4
Cooking Time: 6 Minutes

Ingredients:

- 4 graham cracker sheets
- 4 marshmallows
- 4 teaspoons chunky peanut butter
- 4 ounces dark chocolate
- ½ teaspoon ground cinnamon

Directions:

1. Preheat the air fryer to 390°F. Break the graham crackers in half so you have 8 pieces.
2. Place 4 pieces of graham cracker on the bottom of the air fryer. Top each with one of the marshmallows and bake for 6 or 7 minutes, or until the marshmallows have a golden brown center.
3. While cooking, slather each of the remaining graham crackers with 1 teaspoon peanut butter.
4. When baking completes, carefully remove each of the graham crackers, add 1 ounce of dark chocolate on top of the marshmallow, and lightly sprinkle with cinnamon. Top with the remaining peanut butter graham cracker to make the sandwich. Serve immediately.

Bananas Foster Bread Pudding

Servings: 4
Cooking Time: 25 Minutes

Ingredients:

- ½ cup brown sugar
- 3 eggs
- ¾ cup half and half
- 1 teaspoon pure vanilla extract
- 6 cups cubed Kings Hawaiian bread (½-inch cubes), ½ pound
- 2 bananas, sliced
- 1 cup caramel sauce, plus more for serving

Directions:

1. Preheat the air fryer to 350°F.
2. Combine the brown sugar, eggs, half and half and vanilla extract in a large bowl, whisking until the sugar has dissolved and the mixture is smooth. Stir in the cubed bread and toss to coat all the cubes evenly. Let the bread sit for 10 minutes to absorb the liquid.
3. Mix the sliced bananas and caramel sauce together in a separate bowl.
4. Fill the bottom of 4 (8-ounce) greased ramekins with half the bread cubes. Divide the caramel and bananas between the ramekins, spooning them on top of the bread cubes. Top with the remaining bread cubes and wrap each ramekin with aluminum foil, tenting the foil at the top to leave some room for the bread to puff up during the cooking process.
5. Air-fry two bread puddings at a time for 25 minutes. Let the puddings cool a little and serve warm with additional caramel sauce drizzled on top. A scoop of vanilla ice cream would be nice too and in keeping with our Bananas Foster theme!

Sweet Potato Donut Holes

Servings: 18
Cooking Time: 4 Minutes Per Batch

Ingredients:

- 1 cup flour
- ⅓ cup sugar
- ¼ teaspoon baking soda
- 1 teaspoon baking powder
- ⅛ teaspoon salt
- ½ cup cooked mashed purple sweet potatoes
- 1 egg, beaten
- 2 tablespoons butter, melted
- 1 teaspoon pure vanilla extract
- oil for misting or cooking spray

Directions:

1. Preheat air fryer to 390°F.
2. In a large bowl, stir together the flour, sugar, baking soda, baking powder, and salt.
3. In a separate bowl, combine the potatoes, egg, butter, and vanilla and mix well.
4. Add potato mixture to dry ingredients and stir into a soft dough.
5. Shape dough into 1½-inch balls. Mist lightly with oil or cooking spray.
6. Place 9 donut holes in air fryer basket, leaving a little space in between. Cook for 4 minutes, until done in center and lightly browned outside.
7. Repeat step 6 to cook remaining donut holes.

Banana-lemon Bars

Servings: 6
Cooking Time: 40 Minutes
Ingredients:

- ¾ cup flour
- 2 tbsp powdered sugar
- ¼ cup coconut oil, melted
- ½ cup brown sugar
- 1 tbsp lemon zest
- ¼ cup lemon juice
- ⅛ tsp salt
- ¼ cup mashed bananas
- 1¾ tsp cornstarch
- ¾ tsp baking powder

Directions:

1. Combine the flour, powdered sugar, and coconut oil in a bowl. Place in the fridge. Mix the brown sugar, lemon zest and juice, salt, bananas, cornstarch, and baking powder in a bowl. Stir well. Preheat air fryer to 350°F. Spray a baking pan with oil. Remove the crust from the fridge and press it into the bottom of the pan to form a crust. Place in the air fryer and Bake for 5 minutes or until firm. Remove and spread the lemon filling over the crust. Bake for 18-20 minutes or until the top is golden. Cool for an hour in the fridge. Once firm and cooled, cut into pieces and serve.

Mango Cobbler With Raspberries

Servings: 4
Cooking Time: 30 Minutes
Ingredients:

- 1 ½ cups chopped mango
- 1 cup raspberries
- 1 tbsp brown sugar
- 2 tsp cornstarch
- 1 tsp lemon juice
- 2 tbsp sunflower oil
- 1 tbsp maple syrup
- 1 tsp vanilla
- ½ cup rolled oats
- 1/3 cup flour
- 3 tbsp coconut sugar
- 1 tsp cinnamon
- ¼ tsp nutmeg
- ⅛ tsp salt

Directions:

1. Place the mango, raspberries, brown sugar, cornstarch, and lemon juice in a baking pan. Stir with a rubber spatula until combined. Set aside.
2. In a separate bowl, add the oil, maple syrup, and vanilla and stir well. Toss in the oats, flour, coconut sugar, cinnamon, nutmeg, and salt. Stir until combined. Sprinkle evenly over the mango-raspberry filling. Preheat air fryer to 320°F. Bake for 20 minutes or until the topping is crispy and golden. Enjoy warm.

Fast Brownies

Servings: 4
Cooking Time: 25 Minutes
Ingredients:

- ½ cup flour
- 2 tbsp cocoa
- 1/3 cup granulated sugar
- ¼ tsp baking soda
- 3 tbsp butter, melted
- 1 egg
- ¼ tsp salt
- ½ cup chocolate chips
- ¼ cup chopped hazelnuts
- 1 tbsp powdered sugar
- 1 tsp vanilla extract

Directions:

1. Preheat air fryer at 350°F. Combine all ingredients, except chocolate chips, hazelnuts, and powdered sugar, in a bowl. Fold in chocolate chips and pecans. Press mixture into a greased cake pan. Place cake pan in the frying basket and Bake for 12 minutes. Let cool for 10 minutes before slicing into 9 brownies. Scatter with powdered sugar and serve.

Baked Caramelized Peaches

Servings: 6
Cooking Time: 25 Minutes
Ingredients:

- 3 pitted peaches, halved
- 2 tbsp brown sugar
- 1 cup heavy cream
- 1 tsp vanilla extract
- ¼ tsp ground cinnamon
- 1 cup fresh blueberries

Directions:

1. Preheat air fryer to 380°F. Lay the peaches in the frying basket with the cut side up, then top them with brown sugar. Bake for 7-11 minutes, allowing the peaches to brown around the edges. In a mixing bowl, whisk heavy cream, vanilla, and cinnamon until stiff peaks form. Fold the peaches into a plate. Spoon the cream mixture into the peach cups, top with blueberries, and serve.

Lemon Pound Cake Bites

Servings: 6
Cooking Time: 20 Minutes
Ingredients:

- 1 pound cake, cubed
- 1/3 cup cinnamon sugar
- ½ stick butter, melted
- 1 cup vanilla yogurt
- 3 tbsp brown sugar
- 1 tsp lemon zest

Directions:

1. Preheat the air fryer to 350°F. Drizzle the cake cubes with melted butter, then put them in the cinnamon sugar and toss until coated. Put them in a single layer in the frying basket and Air Fry for 4 minutes or until golden. Remove and place on a serving plate. Combine the yogurt, brown sugar, and lemon zest in a bowl. Serve with the cake bites.

Hasselback Apple Crisp

Servings: 4
Cooking Time: 20 Minutes
Ingredients:

- 2 large Gala apples, peeled, cored and cut in half
- ¼ cup butter, melted
- ½ teaspoon ground cinnamon
- 2 tablespoons sugar
- Topping
- 3 tablespoons butter, melted
- 2 tablespoons brown sugar
- ¼ cup chopped pecans
- 2 tablespoons rolled oats*
- 1 tablespoon flour*
- vanilla ice cream
- caramel sauce

Directions:

1. Place the apples cut side down on a cutting board. Slicing from stem end to blossom end, make 8 to 10 slits down the apple halves but only slice three quarters of the way through the apple, not all the way through to the cutting board.
2. Preheat the air fryer to 330°F and pour a little water into the bottom of the air fryer drawer. (This will help prevent the grease that drips into the bottom drawer from burning and smoking.)
3. Transfer the apples to the air fryer basket, flat side down. Combine ¼ cup of melted butter, cinnamon and sugar in a small bowl. Brush this butter mixture onto the apples and air-fry at 330°F for 15 minutes. Baste the apples several times with the butter mixture during the cooking process.
4. While the apples are air-frying, make the filling. Combine 3 tablespoons of melted butter with the brown sugar, pecans, rolled oats and flour in a bowl. Stir with a fork until the mixture resembles small crumbles.
5. When the timer on the air fryer is up, spoon the topping down the center of the apples. Air-fry at 330°F for an additional 5 minutes.
6. Transfer the apples to a serving plate and serve with vanilla ice cream and caramel sauce.

Giant Buttery Chocolate Chip Cookie

Servings: 4
Cooking Time: 16 Minutes
Ingredients:

- ⅔ cup plus 1 tablespoon All-purpose flour
- ¼ teaspoon Baking soda
- ¼ teaspoon Table salt
- Baking spray (see the headnote)
- 4 tablespoons (¼ cup/½ stick) plus 1 teaspoon Butter, at room temperature
- ¼ cup plus 1 teaspoon Packed dark brown sugar
- 3 tablespoons plus 1 teaspoon Granulated white sugar
- 2½ tablespoons Pasteurized egg substitute, such as Egg Beaters
- ½ teaspoon Vanilla extract
- ¾ cup plus 1 tablespoon Semisweet or bittersweet chocolate chips

Directions:

1. Preheat the air fryer to 350°F .
2. Whisk the flour, baking soda, and salt in a bowl until well combined.
3. For a small air fryer, coat the inside of a 6-inch round cake pan with baking spray. For a medium air fryer, coat the inside of a 7-inch round cake pan with baking spray. And for a large air fryer, coat the inside of an 8-inch round cake pan with baking spray.
4. Using a hand electric mixer at medium speed, beat the butter, brown sugar, and granulated white sugar in a bowl until smooth and thick, about 3 minutes, scraping down the inside of the bowl several times.
5. Beat in the pasteurized egg substitute or egg (as applicable) and vanilla until uniform. Scrape down and remove the beaters. Fold in the flour mixture and chocolate chips with a rubber spatula, just until

combined. Scrape and gently press this dough into the prepared pan, getting it even across the pan to the perimeter.
6. Set the pan in the basket and air-fry undisturbed for 16 minutes, or until the cookie is puffed, browned, and feels set to the touch.
7. Transfer the pan to a wire rack and cool for 10 minutes. Loosen the cookie from the perimeter with a spatula, then invert the pan onto a cutting board and let the cookie come free. Remove the pan and reinvert the cookie onto the wire rack. Cool for 5 minutes more before slicing into wedges to serve.

Oatmeal Blackberry Crisp

Servings: 6
Cooking Time: 20 Minutes

Ingredients:

- 1 cup rolled oats
- ½ cup flour
- ¼ cup olive oil
- ¼ tsp salt
- 1 tsp cinnamon
- 1/3 cup honey
- 4 cups blackberries

Directions:

1. Preheat air fryer to 350°F. Combine rolled oats, flour, olive oil, salt, cinnamon, and honey in a large bowl. Mix well. Spread blackberries on the bottom of a greased cooking pan. Cover them with the oat mixture. Place pan in air fryer and Bake for 15 minutes. Cool for a few minutes. Serve and enjoy.

Air-fried Strawberry Hand Tarts

Servings: 9
Cooking Time: 9 Minutes

Ingredients:

- ½ cup butter, softened
- ½ cup sugar
- 2 eggs
- 1 teaspoon vanilla extract
- 2 tablespoons lemon zest
- 2½ cups all-purpose flour
- 1 teaspoon baking powder
- ¼ teaspoon salt
- 1¼ cups strawberry jam, divided
- 1 egg white, beaten
- 1 cup powdered sugar
- 2 teaspoons milk

Directions:

1. Combine the butter and sugar in a bowl and beat with an electric mixer until the mixture is light and fluffy. Add the eggs one at a time. Add the vanilla extract and lemon zest and mix well. In a separate bowl, combine the flour, baking powder and salt. Add the dry ingredients to the wet ingredients, mixing just until the dough comes together. Transfer the dough to a floured surface and knead by hand for 10 minutes. Cover with a clean kitchen towel and let the dough rest for 30 minutes. (Alternatively, dough can be mixed and kneaded in a stand mixer.)
2. Divide the dough in half and roll each half out into a ¼-inch thick rectangle that measures 12-inches x 9-inches. Cut each rectangle of dough into nine 4-inch x 3-inch rectangles (a pizza cutter is very helpful for this task). You should have 18 rectangles. Spread two teaspoons of strawberry jam in the center of nine of the rectangles leaving a ¼-inch border around the edges. Brush the egg white around the edges of each rectangle and top with the remaining nine rectangles of dough. Press the back of a fork around the edges to seal the tarts shut. Brush the top of the tarts with the beaten egg white and pierce the dough three or four times down the center of the tart with a fork.
3. Preheat the air fryer to 350°F.
4. Air-fry the tarts in batches at 350°F for 6 minutes. Flip the tarts over and air-fry for an additional 3 minutes.
5. While the tarts are air-frying, make the icing. Combine the powdered sugar, ¼ cup strawberry preserves and milk in a bowl, whisking until the icing is smooth. Spread the icing over the top of each tart, leaving an empty border around the edges. Decorate with sprinkles if desired.

Fried Pineapple Chunks

Servings: 3
Cooking Time: 10 Minutes
Ingredients:

- 3 tablespoons Cornstarch
- 1 Large egg white, beaten until foamy
- 1 cup (4 ounces) Ground vanilla wafer cookies (not low-fat cookies)
- 1/4 teaspoon Ground dried ginger
- 18 (about 2 1/4 cups) Fresh 1-inch chunks peeled and cored pineapple

Directions:

1. Preheat the air fryer to 400°F.
2. Put the cornstarch in a medium or large bowl. Put the beaten egg white in a small bowl. Pour the cookie crumbs and ground dried ginger into a large zip-closed plastic bag, shaking it a bit to combine them.
3. Dump the pineapple chunks into the bowl with the cornstarch. Toss and stir until well coated. Use your cleaned fingers or a large fork like a shovel to pick up a few pineapple chunks, shake off any excess cornstarch, and put them in the bowl with the egg white. Stir gently, then pick them up and let any excess egg white slip back into the rest. Put them in the bag with the crumb mixture. Repeat the cornstarch-then-egg process until all the pineapple chunks are in the bag. Seal the bag and shake gently, turning the bag this way and that, to coat the pieces well.
4. Set the coated pineapple chunks in the basket with as much air space between them as possible. Even a fraction of an inch will work, but they should not touch. Air-fry undisturbed for 10 minutes, or until golden brown and crisp.
5. Gently dump the contents of the basket onto a wire rack. Cool for at least 5 minutes or up to 15 minutes before serving.

Fried Twinkies

Servings:6
Cooking Time: 5 Minutes
Ingredients:

- 2 Large egg white(s)
- 2 tablespoons Water
- 1 1/2 cups (about 9 ounces) Ground gingersnap cookie crumbs
- 6 Twinkies
- Vegetable oil spray

Directions:

1. Preheat the air fryer to 400°F.
2. Set up and fill two shallow soup plates or small pie plates on your counter: one for the egg white(s), whisked with the water until foamy; and one for the gingersnap crumbs.
3. Dip a Twinkie in the egg white(s), turning it to coat on all sides, even the ends. Let the excess egg white mixture slip back into the rest, then set the Twinkie in the crumbs. Roll it to coat on all sides, even the ends, pressing gently to get an even coating. Then repeat this process: egg white(s), followed by crumbs. Lightly coat the prepared Twinkie on all sides with vegetable oil spray. Set aside and coat each of the remaining Twinkies with the same double-dipping technique, followed by spraying.
4. Set the Twinkies flat side up in the basket with as much air space between them as possible. Air-fry for 5 minutes, or until browned and crunchy.
5. Use a nonstick-safe spatula to gently transfer the Twinkies to a wire rack. Cool for at least 10 minutes before serving.

Giant Oatmeal–peanut Butter Cookie

Servings: 4
Cooking Time: 18 Minutes
Ingredients:

- 1 cup Rolled oats (not quick-cooking or steel-cut oats)
- 1/2 cup All-purpose flour
- 1/2 teaspoon Ground cinnamon
- 1/2 teaspoon Baking soda
- 1/3 cup Packed light brown sugar
- 1/4 cup Solid vegetable shortening
- 2 tablespoons Natural-style creamy peanut butter
- 3 tablespoons Granulated white sugar
- 2 tablespoons (or 1 small egg, well beaten) Pasteurized egg substitute, such as Egg Beaters
- 1/3 cup Roasted, salted peanuts, chopped
- Baking spray

Directions:

1. Preheat the air fryer to 350°F .
2. Stir the oats, flour, cinnamon, and baking soda in a bowl until well combined.
3. Using an electric hand mixer at medium speed, beat the brown sugar, shortening, peanut butter, granulated white sugar, and egg substitute or egg (as applicable) until smooth and creamy, about 3 minutes, scraping down the inside of the bowl occasionally.

4. Scrape down and remove the beaters. Fold in the flour mixture and peanuts with a rubber spatula just until all the flour is moistened and the peanut bits are evenly distributed in the dough.
5. For a small air fryer, coat the inside of a 6-inch round cake pan with baking spray. For a medium air fryer, coat the inside of a 7-inch round cake pan with baking spray. And for a large air fryer, coat the inside of an 8-inch round cake pan with baking spray. Scrape and gently press the dough into the prepared pan, spreading it into an even layer to the perimeter.
6. Set the pan in the basket and air-fry undisturbed for 18 minutes, or until well browned.
7. Transfer the pan to a wire rack and cool for 15 minutes. Loosen the cookie from the perimeter with a spatula, then invert the pan onto a cutting board and let the cookie come free. Remove the pan and reinvert the cookie onto the wire rack. Cool for 5 minutes more before slicing into wedges to serve.

Fall Caramelized Apples

Servings: 2
Cooking Time: 25 Minutes
Ingredients:

- 2 apples, sliced
- 1 ½ tsp brown sugar
- ¼ tsp cinnamon
- ¼ tsp nutmeg
- ¼ tsp salt
- 1 tsp lemon zest

Directions:

1. Preheat air fryer to 390°F. Set the apples upright in a baking pan. Add 2 tbsp of water to the bottom to keep the apples moist. Sprinkle the tops with sugar, lemon zest, cinnamon, and nutmeg. Lightly sprinkle the halves with salt and the tops with oil. Bake for 20 minutes or until the apples are tender and golden on top. Enjoy.

Vanilla Cupcakes With Chocolate Chips

Servings: 2
Cooking Time: 25 Minutes + Cooling Time
Ingredients:

- ½ cup white sugar
- 1 ½ cups flour
- 2 tsp baking powder
- ½ tsp salt
- 2/3 cup sunflower oil
- 1 egg
- 2 tsp maple extract
- ¼ cup vanilla yogurt
- 1 cup chocolate chips

Directions:

1. Preheat air fryer to 350°F. Combine the sugar, flour, baking powder, and salt in a bowl and stir to combine. Whisk the egg in a separate bowl. Pour in the sunflower oil, yogurt, and maple extract, and continue whisking until light and fluffy. Spoon the wet mixture into the dry ingredients and stir to combine. Gently fold in the chocolate chips with a spatula. Divide the batter between cupcake cups and Bake in the air fryer for 12-15 minutes or until a toothpick comes out dry. Remove the cupcakes let them cool. Serve.

Coconut Crusted Bananas With Pineapple Sauce

Servings: 4
Cooking Time: 5 Minutes
Ingredients:

- Pineapple Sauce
- 1½ cups puréed fresh pineapple
- 2 tablespoons sugar
- juice of 1 lemon
- ¼ teaspoon ground cinnamon
- 3 firm bananas
- ¼ cup sweetened condensed milk
- 1¼ cups shredded coconut
- ⅓ cup crushed graham crackers (crumbs)*
- vegetable or canola oil, in a spray bottle
- vanilla frozen yogurt or ice cream

Directions:

1. Make the pineapple sauce by combining the pineapple, sugar, lemon juice and cinnamon in a saucepan. Simmer the mixture on the stovetop for 20 minutes, and then set it aside.
2. Slice the bananas diagonally into ½-inch thick slices and place them in a bowl. Pour the sweetened condensed milk into the bowl and toss the bananas gently to coat. Combine the coconut and graham cracker crumbs together in a shallow dish. Remove the banana slices from the condensed milk and let any excess milk drip off. Dip the banana slices in the coconut and crumb mixture to coat both sides. Spray the coated slices with oil.
3. Preheat the air fryer to 400°F.
4. Grease the bottom of the air fryer basket with a little oil. Air-fry the bananas in batches at 400°F for 5 minutes, turning them over halfway through the cooking time. Air-fry until the bananas are golden brown on both sides.
5. Serve warm over vanilla frozen yogurt with some of the pineapple sauce spooned over top.

Banana-almond Delights

Servings: 4
Cooking Time: 30 Minutes

Ingredients:

- 1 ripe banana, mashed
- 1 tbsp almond liqueur
- ½ tsp ground cinnamon
- 2 tbsp coconut sugar
- 1 cup almond flour
- ¼ tsp baking soda
- 8 raw almonds

Directions:

1. Preheat air fryer to 300°F. Add the banana to a bowl and stir in almond liqueur, cinnamon, and coconut sugar until well combined. Toss in almond flour and baking soda until smooth. Make 8 balls out of the mixture. Place the balls onto the parchment-lined frying basket, flatten each into ½-inch thick, and press 1 almond into the center. Bake for 12 minutes, turn and Bake for 6 more minutes. Let cool slightly before serving.

Choco-granola Bars With Cranberries

Servings: 6
Cooking Time: 20 Minutes

Ingredients:

- 2 tbsp dark chocolate chunks
- 2 cups quick oats
- 2 tbsp dried cranberries
- 3 tbsp shredded coconut
- ½ cup maple syrup
- 1 tsp ground cinnamon
- ⅛ tsp salt
- 2 tbsp smooth peanut butter

Directions:

1. Preheat air fryer to 360°F. Stir together all the ingredients in a bowl until well combined. Press the oat mixture into a parchment-lined baking pan in a single layer. Put the pan into the frying basket and Bake for 15 minutes. Remove the pan from the fryer, and lift the granola cake out of the pan using the edges of the parchment paper. Leave to cool for 5 minutes. Serve sliced and enjoy!.

Peanut Butter S'mores

Servings:10
Cooking Time: 1 Minute

Ingredients:

- 10 Graham crackers (full, double-square cookies as they come out of the package)
- 5 tablespoons Natural-style creamy or crunchy peanut butter
- ½ cup Milk chocolate chips
- 10 Standard-size marshmallows (not minis and not jumbo campfire ones)

Directions:

1. Preheat the air fryer to 350°F .
2. Break the graham crackers in half widthwise at the marked place, so the rectangle is now in two squares. Set half of the squares flat side up on your work surface. Spread each with about 1½ teaspoons peanut butter, then set 10 to 12 chocolate chips point side up into the peanut butter on each, pressing gently so the chips stick.
3. Flatten a marshmallow between your clean, dry hands and set it atop the chips. Do the same with the remaining marshmallows on the other coated graham crackers. Do not set the other half of the graham crackers on top of these coated graham crackers.
4. When the machine is at temperature, set the treats graham cracker side down in a single layer in the basket. They may touch, but even a fraction of an inch between them will provide better air flow. Air-fry undisturbed for 45 seconds.
5. Use a nonstick-safe spatula to transfer the topped graham crackers to a wire rack. Set the other graham cracker squares flat side down over the marshmallows. Cool for a couple of minutes before serving.

Brownies With White Chocolate

Servings: 6
Cooking Time: 30 Minutes

Ingredients:

- ¼ cup white chocolate chips
- ¼ cup muscovado sugar
- 1 egg
- 2 tbsp white sugar
- 2 tbsp canola oil
- 1 tsp vanilla
- ¼ cup cocoa powder
- 1/3 cup flour

Directions:

1. Preheat air fryer to 340°F. Beat the egg with muscovado sugar and white sugar in a bowl. Mix in the canola oil and vanilla. Next, stir in cocoa powder and flour until just combined. Gently fold in white chocolate chips. Spoon the batter into a lightly pan. Bake until the brownies are set when lightly touched on top, about 20 minutes. Let to cool completely before slicing.

Fried Cannoli Wontons

Servings: 10
Cooking Time: 8 Minutes

Ingredients:

- 8 ounces Neufchâtel cream cheese
- 1/4 cup powdered sugar
- 1 teaspoon vanilla extract
- 1/4 teaspoon salt
- 1/4 cup mini chocolate chips
- 2 tablespoons chopped pecans (optional)
- 20 wonton wrappers
- 1/4 cup filtered water

Directions:

1. Preheat the air fryer to 370°F.
2. In a large bowl, use a hand mixer to combine the cream cheese with the powdered sugar, vanilla, and salt. Fold in the chocolate chips and pecans. Set aside.
3. Lay the wonton wrappers out on a flat, smooth surface and place a bowl with the filtered water next to them.
4. Use a teaspoon to evenly divide the cream cheese mixture among the 20 wonton wrappers, placing the batter in the center of the wontons.
5. Wet the tip of your index finger, and gently moisten the outer edges of the wrapper. Then fold each wrapper until it creates a secure pocket.
6. Liberally spray the air fryer basket with olive oil mist.
7. Place the wontons into the basket, and cook for 5 to 8 minutes. When the outer edges begin to brown, remove the wontons from the air fryer basket. Repeat cooking with remaining wontons.
8. Serve warm.

Carrot Cake With Cream Cheese Icing

Servings: 6
Cooking Time: 55 Minutes

Ingredients:

- 1 1/4 cups all-purpose flour
- 1 teaspoon baking powder
- 1/2 teaspoon baking soda
- 1 teaspoon ground cinnamon
- 1/4 teaspoon ground nutmeg
- 1/4 teaspoon salt
- 2 cups grated carrot (about 3 to 4 medium carrots or 2 large)
- 3/4 cup granulated sugar
- 1/4 cup brown sugar
- 2 eggs
- 3/4 cup canola or vegetable oil
- For the icing:
- 8 ounces cream cheese, softened at room , Temperature: 8 tablespoons butter (4 ounces or 1 stick), softened at room , Temperature: 1 cup powdered sugar
- 1 teaspoon pure vanilla extract

Directions:

1. Grease a 7-inch cake pan.
2. Combine the flour, baking powder, baking soda, cinnamon, nutmeg and salt in a bowl. Add the grated carrots and toss well. In a separate bowl, beat the sugars and eggs together until light and frothy. Drizzle in the oil, beating constantly. Fold the egg mixture into the dry ingredients until everything is just combined and you no longer see any traces of flour. Pour the batter into the cake pan and wrap the pan completely in greased aluminum foil.
3. Preheat the air fryer to 350°F.
4. Lower the cake pan into the air fryer basket using a sling made of aluminum foil (fold a piece of aluminum foil into a strip about 2-inches wide by 24-inches long). Fold the ends of the aluminum foil into the air fryer, letting them rest on top of the cake. Air-fry for 40 minutes. Remove the aluminum foil cover and air-fry for an additional 15 minutes or until a skewer inserted into the center of the cake comes out clean and the top is nicely browned.
5. While the cake is cooking, beat the cream cheese, butter, powdered sugar and vanilla extract together using a hand mixer, stand mixer or food processor (or a lot of elbow grease!).
6. Remove the cake pan from the air fryer and let the cake cool in the cake pan for 10 minutes or so. Then remove the cake from the pan and let it continue to cool completely. Frost the cake with the cream cheese icing and serve.

RECIPES INDEX

T

V

W

Y

Z

Printed in Great Britain
by Amazon

20121346R00066